What People Are Saying A

Weekly Prayer Ser
for Teenagers

"This book is a treasure for youth ministers and teachers. Sr. Valerie Schneider's creative prayer services connect Scripture to the real lives of young people in ways that can shape their faith while deeply moving their hearts."

Patricia H. Livingston
Counselor, Speaker, author of Lessons of the Heart

"Scripture comes alive in *Weekly Prayer Services for Teenagers* where young people are challenged to turn the ordinary into grace-filled moments and events! Once again, Sr. Valerie has touched the realities of teen life and made them holy."

Sr. Mary Janeta Stamper, SND
Past Principal and Junior High Teacher

"Sister Valerie Schneider has provided youth ministers and those who work with high school students valuable, action-oriented, and creative prayer services for a journey through the church year. The wide variety of themes and celebrations allow for flexibility and creativity within any youth ministry program."

Michael D. Ausperk
Pastor of Saint Agnes Church and
Chaplain of Elyria Catholic High School, Elyria, OH
Author, *Teenagers Come and Pray!*

"Every Friday my seventh grade teacher prepared us for the Sunday liturgy by having us copy the Gospel into a special notebook. If only she had had Sister Valerie's book to make the Sunday readings come alive! We would have been praying, discussing, and doing all kinds of engaging activities to help us take to heart and remember God's weekly Good News. Today's catechists are fortunate to have such a creative resource to implement completely or to dip into for good ideas."

Mary Kathleen Glavich
Author, *Leading Students into Scripture*
and *Weekday Liturgies for Children*

"If you are looking for excellent material for prayer services with teens, this is it. Each week the lectionary passages are prepared for several readers to proclaim. Surrounding the Scripture are prayers, reflections, and activities designed to involve students in connecting the gospel to their own life experience. The language is down to earth, the tone deeply affirming as well as challenging. This collection is both inspiring and practical, a very fine resource for praying with young people."

Patricia H. Livingston
Livingston Associates, Tampa, FL

"*Weekly Prayer Services for Teenagers* helps religious educators to meet the need to guide the young in an intelligent prayer life. The fire of faith in the services provides the wind of God's spirit. As the young people read the gospel, they are engaged by the leader in a reflection on its challenge or support in their daily lives. The activities bolster the theme of each service and help the young people to internalize the gospel's message. *Weekly Prayer Services for Teenagers* is a winner, a gift to teacher and student alike!"

Kevin Regan
Author, 20 *Teen Prayer Services and*
20 More Teen Prayer Services

"Religion teachers, catechists, and youth ministers will find these prayer services corresponding to the liturgical weeks of Years C and A a very useful teaching tool. With the same flexible format as in the first two editions, Sr. Valerie addresses many life issues that teenagers face today and helps them find meaning through Scripture, reflection, activities, and prayer.

"I am pleased that one of our excellent high-school teachers has made a significant contribution to this need for weekly prayer based on the lectionary."

Sr. Janet Doyle, O.P.
Director, Catholic Youth and School Services
Diocese of Toledo

"Sr. Valerie travels the Emmaus road with teens inviting them to recall the words of Jesus. By shared reading of each Sunday's gospel, students hear Jesus' words in the familiar voices of credible peers. Respectful questions inviting personal responses and shared experiences spark young hearts to glow as they discover a new Jesus in their lives. The road question 'What things?' of the Emmaus stranger gets reworked skillfully by Sr. Valerie, and the rest is grace."

+ Robert W. Donnelly
Auxiliary Bishop of Toledo

Weekly Prayer Services

for TEENAGERS

LECTIONARY-BASED for the SCHOOL YEAR

Years C and A

M. Valerie Schneider, SND

TWENTY-THIRD PUBLICATIONS

Mystic, CT 06355

Twenty-Third Publications
185 Willow Street
P.O. Box 180
Mystic, CT 06355
(860) 536-2611
(800) 321-0411

ISBN 0-89622-929-7
Library of Congress Catalog Card Number 98-60307
Printed in the U.S.A.

Dedication

*In thanksgiving
for the gifts of the Holy Spirit*

Contents

Weekly Prayer Services for Teenagers

Introduction

The forty prayer services in this volume, corresponding to the liturgical weeks of Years C and A in the lectionary cycle that spans the academic year, September through May, are intended for junior and senior high school students, whether in a Catholic school or a religious education program. These services involve the teens in a dramatic reading of the upcoming Sunday gospel, questions for reflection and discussion, some communal prayer, and an activity—all related to a theme associated with the lectionary reading for the Sunday.

(A prayer service for All Saints Day is included, because in 1998 this feast falls on a Sunday. The prayer service for the Thirty-First Sunday in Ordinary Time is also included for the next time it is needed.)

The format of the services contains these elements: 1) the theme, 2) materials needed for the optional activities, 3) a call to prayer, 4) a reading of the gospel, dramatized to be read by several participants, 5) reflection and discussion questions, 6) one or more optional activities that can be done within the context of the service, at another time, or omitted, and 7) a closing prayer.

Over the academic year the teens will be exposed to a variety of themes: discipleship, social justice, prayer, gratitude, self-image, saints, human potential, morality, the new millennium, risktaking, union with God, mystical experiences, worship, and others. By participating in these services in the week before the Sunday liturgy, the teens will be primed for, and more attentive to, the proclamation of the Scripture that day.

The activities are directed to the students. The leader, perhaps together with the students, may decide whether the activities are to be performed as part of the prayer service or at a later time, if at all. Omitting or postponing the activities will not detract from the prayer service.

The prayer services could be used to begin or end religion classes at the junior or senior high school levels or to surround the religion class (using Call to Prayer and Reading at the beginning of class and Closing Prayer at the end of class). Those involved in the Order of Christian Initiation (RCIA) may find segments or whole prayer services helpful to their own lectionary-based programs. The services could also be used independently of lectionary-based programs whenever the gospel fits the curriculum or whenever a church or school staff member needs a prayer service for a particular season or feast.

The purpose of *Weekly Prayer Services for Teenagers* is to help Christian teens live their baptismal calling. In any way this book can be helpful to that end, please feel free to photocopy or adapt.

May we preach the gospel with our lips and our lives!

Close Followers of Christ

Theme

Dedicated followers of Christ don't calculate the cost; they go the whole way with the Lord—even to Calvary.

Materials Needed

Background music, Bibles for each student

Call to Prayer

LEADER Lord Jesus Christ, we come before you, not so much as students and teachers but as followers. We want to learn, but above all we want to live your life.

ALL Help us put the Good News before good marks.

LEADER Lord Jesus Christ, we want to succeed, but we are more concerned about being your followers.

ALL Help us put the race to eternal life before athletic and academic competition.

LEADER We want to be a united class, but we realize it's more important to be church.

ALL Help us build our unity on shared prayer and service performed together.

LEADER Lord Jesus Christ, while we hope for many fun times, we remember that suffering is part of being your disciple.

ALL Help us put the needs of the world before our personal wants.

Reading (Luke 14:25–33)

READER 1 Now large crowds were traveling with Jesus, and he turned and said to them, "Whoever comes to me and does not hate father and mother, wife and children, brothers and sisters, yes, and even life itself, cannot be my disciple. Whoever does not carry the cross and follow me cannot be my disciple.

READER 2 "For which of you, intending to build a tower, does not first sit down and estimate the cost, to see whether he has enough to complete it? Otherwise, when he has laid a foundation and is not able to finish, all who see it will begin to ridicule him, saying, 'This fellow began to build and was not able to finish.'

READER 3 "Or what king, going out to wage war against another king, will not sit down first and consider whether he is able with ten thousand to oppose the one who comes against him with twenty thousand? If he cannot, then, while the other is still far away, he sends a delegation and asks for the terms of peace.

READER 4 "So therefore, none of you can become my disciple if you do not give up all your possessions."

Reflection

LEADER We begin the new academic year with a definite message: follow Christ closely. Because Luke uses the Greek word *bastazo* (to carry), which John uses of Jesus on the way to Calvary, the message is unmistakable: expect a close, near literal, following of Jesus even in suffering. Are we a distant follower who makes sure Calvary stays on the far horizon, or are we such a close follower that we forget to calculate the costs of discipleship? Jesus demands total dedication.

Unlike Christ who carried the cross on his shoulders, we followers carry the death of Jesus in our bodies (2 Cor 4:10). We have been crucified with Christ, and now Christ lives in us (Gal 2:20). Are we so much like Christ that we take his stance toward people; for example, do we identify with the poor? Are we so much like Christ that we give up our possessions? Are we so much like Christ that we will risk our reputation as we do the right thing? Are we so much like Christ that we live life passionately without calculating the outcome of every decision? Do we expect some trouble for our self-dedication?

God wants everything from us. What are the hardest things to give God?

Jesus doesn't want us to calculate the cost of discipleship. When do you find yourself saying, in effect, "Well, I'll go this far in following Christ, but no farther" or "I'll give you this much, Jesus, but don't expect anything more"?

Did your discipleship make your past summer vacation harder, easier, or no different? What do you think will be the most challenging aspects of discipleship in the coming academic year?

Activities (choose one)

1. Ask God to give a message to your class. Then open the Bible randomly. Share the message God seems to be addressing to the class. (Background music may be helpful.) Does there seem to be a common thread running through all the passages? If so, post the message and refer to it often throughout the coming year. Or write each message on a card and use the cards to formulate prayers to begin classes.

2. Because discipleship requires difficult things, discuss one sacrifice that you

could perform as a class throughout the coming year; for example, collect for the needy, perform free service, or work with an organization devoted to social justice.

Closing Prayer

LEADER   This year we must become Christians in the full sense of the phrase, followers of Christ.

RIGHT   Lord Jesus Christ, we hear your gentle voice say, Follow me.

LEFT   Help us be followers who don't count the cost of discipleship.

RIGHT   Lord Jesus Christ, you are the Light of the World.

LEFT   Help us share your light, bringing brightness to those who are sad, lonely, or depressed.

RIGHT   Lord Jesus Christ, you are the way.

LEFT   Help us walk as companions on the way to eternal life.

RIGHT   Lord Jesus Christ, you are food for the journey.

LEFT   Help us become bread for the world.

RIGHT   Lord Jesus Christ, you are forgiveness.

LEFT   Help us forgive ourselves and each other.

RIGHT   Lord Jesus Christ, you are our friend.

LEFT   Help us grow in friendship, for friends who follow you together are strong disciples.

LEADER   Jesus, may we walk with you in all these ways and more. We ask this in the name of the Father and of the Son and of the Holy Spirit.

ALL   Amen.

More Than We Can Imagine

Theme

When we assume responsibility for our problems, there is usually more that can be done to help ourselves than we first imagine. Our trust in God and others will help us go beyond our own resources.

Call to Prayer *(adapted from 1 Timothy 1:12–17)*

LEADER   O God, we are grateful for your abundant mercy and overflowing grace. They are more than we can imagine.

ALL   We believe that Christ came into the world to save us. We praise and thank you, Lord Jesus, for your unimaginable patience toward us, and we say: "To the King of the ages, immortal, invisible, the only God, be honor and glory forever and ever. Amen."

Reading (Luke 15:1–32)

READER 1   Now all the tax collectors and sinners were coming near to listen to him. And the Pharisees and the scribes were grumbling and saying, "This fellow welcomes sinners and eats with them." So he told them this parable:

READER 2   "Which of you, having a hundred sheep and losing one of them, does not leave the ninety-nine in the wilderness and go after the one that is lost until he finds it? When he has found it, he lays it on his shoulders and rejoices. And when he comes home, he calls together his friends and neighbors, saying to them, 'Rejoice with me, for I have found my sheep that was lost.' Just so, I tell you, there will be more joy in heaven over one sinner who repents than over ninety-nine righteous persons who need no repentance.

READER 3   "Or what woman having ten silver coins, if she loses one of them, does not light a lamp, sweep the house, and search carefully until she finds it? When she has found it, she calls together her friends and neighbors, saying, 'Rejoice with me, for I have found the coin that I had lost.' Just so, I tell you, there is joy in the presence of the angels of God over one sinner who repents."

READER 4   Then Jesus said, "There was a man who had two sons. The younger of them said to his father,

READER 5   "'Father, give me the share of the property that will belong to me.'

READER 4 "So he divided his property between them. A few days later the younger son gathered all he had and traveled to a distant country, and there he squandered his property in dissolute living. When he had spent everything, a severe famine took place throughout that country, and he began to be in need. So he went and hired himself out to one of the citizens of that country, who sent him to his fields to feed the pigs. He would gladly have filled himself with the pods that the pigs were eating; and no one gave him anything. But when he came to himself he said,

READER 5 "'How many of my father's hired hands have bread enough and to spare, but here I am dying of hunger! I will get up and go to my father, and I will say to him, Father, I have sinned against heaven and before you; I am no longer worthy to be called your son; treat me like one of your hired hands.'

READER 6 "So he went off and went to his father. But while he was still far off, his father saw him and was filled with compassion; he ran and put his arms around him and kissed him. Then the son said to him,

READER 5 "'Father, I have sinned against heaven and before you; I am no longer worthy to be called your son.'

READER 6 "But the father said to his slaves,

READER 7 "'Quickly, bring out a robe—the best one—and put it on him; put a ring on his finger and sandals on his feet. And get the fatted calf and kill it, and let us eat and celebrate; for this son of mine was dead and is alive again; he was lost and is found!'

READER 6 "And they began to celebrate. Now his elder son was in the field; and when he came and approached the house, he heard music and dancing. He called one of the slaves and asked what was going on. He replied,

READER 8 "'Your brother has come, and your father has killed the fatted calf, because he has got him back safe and sound.'

READER 9 "Then he became angry and refused to go in. His father came out and began to plead with him. But he answered his father,

READER 10 "'Listen! For all these years I have been working like a slave for you, and I have never disobeyed your command; yet you have never given me even a young goat so that I might celebrate with my friends. But when this son of yours came back, who has devoured your property with prostitutes, you killed the fatted calf for him!'

READER 9 "Then the father said to him,

READER 7 "'Son, you are always with me, and all that is mine is yours. But we had to celebrate and rejoice, because this brother of yours was dead and has come to life; he was lost and has been found!'"

Reflection

LEADER The three stories we just read are like a tiny gospel within the gospel. All three begin with a negative situation and end in a positive one—just like the dying and rising of Jesus, the basic kernel of the gospel. They all deal with loss and gain, like the thread of losing ourselves to find ourselves that runs through the gospel. All three could be tragic, yet they end happily, as does the story of salvation, God's plan to let all people live happily forever in the kingdom. The stories are so rich that we could reflect forever, but we will focus on just one aspect; namely, how we need to take responsibility for our situation, do what we can ourselves, but not be afraid to trust others to find solutions better than those we could ever imagine.

The shepherds in the first parable may have blamed themselves or one another for letting a sheep stray, but they solved the problem by letting all but one shepherd take home the ninety-nine, while the last shepherd stayed behind to look for the stray. Working together, trusting each other, they finally had the original one hundred.

The woman with the ten coins lost one, which may have represented a day's wage and the food for the day. She could have hidden her distress, but she trusts others to rejoice with her rather than deride her for carelessness. In the end many persons rejoiced, when the joy could have been limited to one.

The younger son was in a great dilemma: starve or return home to be a hired hand. With trust in his father he returns home to face the consequences of his actions. But the welcome was more than he could ever have imagined! He who squandered half the property was given a ring representing authority over financial matters. He who thought the most he could ask for was slavery was given shoes and a robe, items never worn by slaves. He who thought the rest of his life would be filled with drudgery and shame was given a banquet and a chance for a better tomorrow.

All three stories ask us several related questions: Can you trust that there may be better outcomes if, after taking personal responsibility, you look to others for more solutions? Do you realize that you are not alone; as a Christian, there is always someone else to help you? Can you share another's joy? Are you happy when someone else is successful? If not, why?

Have you ever relied solely on yourself but later discovered that others could have helped you? When we have serious problems, we often want to be left alone. Maybe we don't want anyone else to find out. Yet such isolation can be disastrous. Whom can you trust?

These stories show that God is joyful over a sinner's repentance. Can you participate in the joy or success of others?

Sometimes we put having a good time over responsibilities. Is there any way to become more responsible without curtailing too much fun?

Whose sin was worse: the sin of the younger son's greed and independence or the older son's sin of jealousy and hate? Are the two brothers like two sides of yourself?

Activities (choose one)

1. In three groups write modern versions of these three parables and dramatize them for the rest of the class.

2. Make a list of problems that may beset persons your age. Under each problem list persons and organizations who may help find solutions. You may want to add addresses and phone numbers, then make copies for everyone.

3. Write a note of apology, if you need to do so. Or write, call, or e-mail someone with whom to share some joy.

Closing Prayer

LEADER   Heavenly Father, we are like the prodigal son. See us in the distance. Run to meet us. Give us gifts. Above all, put your arms around us, hug and kiss us, and tell us that it's OK. We feel so bad about who we are, Lord. Tell us we're your very special sons and daughters. Help us hear you say, "All that is mine is yours."

ALL   We praise and thank you, O Father, for our brothers and sisters. Help us to always celebrate and rejoice with them. And we praise and thank you for your great goodness to us. Help us always to turn with confidence to you and to your holy people in our need. We ask this through Christ our Lord, who gave us the stories that let us trust your infinite love. Amen.

Business Cards for This World and the Next

Theme

Our spiritual lives and our physical lives are connected. We cannot separate religious practice from the rest of our lives.

Materials Needed

Index cards to make business cards, pens, markers

Call to Prayer

LEADER Lord, give us the full power of your Holy Spirit so that our faith will make a difference in other people's lives.

ALL Holy Spirit, when we pray, help us to bring to prayer our work and recreation and learning.

LEADER When we work and play, help us bring our prayer to these situations.

ALL When we learn, let our learning have meaning in all the other areas of our lives. Make us whole persons who are comfortable in every facet of life.

LEADER Never let us separate our prayer from our work or our leisure from our learning but rather see everything as one.

ALL Help us to lead Christian lives in every place and at every time, for we are Christians every minute of the day.

Reading (Luke 16:1–13)

READER 1 Then Jesus said to the disciples, "There was a rich man who had a manager, and charges were brought to him that this man was squandering his property. So he summoned him and said to him, 'What is this that I hear about you? Give me an accounting of your management, because you cannot be my manager any longer.'

READER 2 "Then the manager said to himself, 'What will I do, now that my master is taking the position away from me? I am not strong enough to dig, and I am ashamed to beg. I have decided what to do so that, when I am dismissed as manager, people may welcome me into their homes.'

READER 3   "So, summoning his master's debtors one by one, he asked the first, 'How much do you owe my master?' He answered, 'A hundred jugs of olive oil.' He said to him, 'Take your bill, sit down quickly, and make it fifty.'

READER 4   "Then he asked another, 'And how much do you owe?' He replied, 'A hundred containers of wheat.' He said to him, 'Take your bill and make it eighty.'

READER 5   "And his master commended the dishonest manager because he had acted shrewdly; for the children of this age are more shrewd in dealing with their own generation than are the children of light. And I tell you, make friends for yourselves by means of dishonest wealth so that when it is gone, they may welcome you into the eternal homes.

READER 6   "Whoever is faithful in a very little is faithful also in much; and whoever is dishonest in a very little is dishonest also in much. If then you have not been faithful with the dishonest wealth, who will entrust to you the true riches? And if you have not been faithful with what belongs to another, who will give you what is your own? No slave can serve two masters; for a slave will either hate the one and love the other, or be devoted to the one and despise the other. You cannot serve God and wealth."

Reflection

LEADER   Perhaps the manager canceled the excessive profit that he himself would have received as the middleman, a tactic that would have made him dishonest to the extent that his master's security was jeopardized. Because of the moral gray area, the story does not seem to make any exact moral demands on ourselves. We could easily put the story down and tell ourselves, "Just do what you need to do to save your own neck, and that will be all that matters." But Jesus adds a spiritual twist by mentioning "eternal homes," "true riches," and service of God. Going about the "world's" business is not an excuse for ignoring "heaven's" business.

Day to day we constantly have to deal with people: perhaps the student who hurt us, the parent who nags, the sibling who annoys us, the teacher who dislikes us, and the persons with whom we necessarily interact but really don't "meet person-to-person" like employers, bus drivers, store clerks, waitresses, and so on. It's easy to use or manipulate these people for our own ends—and easier yet to ignore them altogether. But stopping to see these people as the Body of Christ transforms the "world's business" to "heavenly business."

Our spiritual lives are not opposed to our physical lives. The only way we can live Christianity is through our bodies. How can the following become Christian actions: (a) ordering a meal in a fast-food restaurant, (b) walking through the school halls, (c) using study halls, (d) attending or participating in a cross-country meet or football game, (e) listening to the car radio?

When we partake of the Body of Christ in the Eucharist, we become the Body of Christ. Communion in the Body of Christ is community in the Body of Christ. How can we treat the following persons as the Body of Christ: (a) parents, (b) principals and teachers, (c) coaches, (d) bus drivers, (e) employers, (f) underclassmen? Who are the persons in your life who would be the most difficult to treat as the Body of Christ? What are the best ways to deal with these persons? What could you do to become more aware of their status as God's children?

Activity

Make a business card that shows your main business is to be a member of the Body of Christ. (Alternative: Make a business card with two sides: one for your desired future career and the other for your spiritual business. Make a logo that fits your earthly and heavenly business.)

Closing Prayer

LEADER   Lord, help us find an ideal, a dream, something important to achieve.

ALL   Inspire us in work and routine, recreation and learning, prayer and service that nothing will be humdrum, but rather a step toward achieving our dreams.

LEADER   Let everything we call "boring" become special, because these things have the potential to develop our characters in the manner of the human character of Jesus Christ.

ALL   Help us to remember to give every activity to you as gift, and let it be done for you, Lord. In this way the most routine becomes a wonderful way to achieve your plan, O God. Amen.

Am I Bothered Enough to Bother?

Theme

As Christians, we cannot be indifferent to need or exclusive of others. Christians cannot afford a "Don't bother me" attitude. We need to help those within our reach.

Call to Prayer

LEADER Heavenly Father, we are so often concerned about our own needs that we fail to see the needs of others. When we are concerned about what we wear,

ALL help us lift up in prayer those who have no shoes.

LEADER When we are concerned about what others will think of our house or car,

ALL help us be aware of the homeless and those who must live in their cars.

LEADER When we are overconcerned with academic or athletic success,

ALL let us remember those whose whole lives seem to be failure.

LEADER When we would rather not bother with anyone outside our own circle of friends,

ALL let us reach out to the lonely. Give us the gift of being bothered enough to bother getting involved.

Reading (Luke 16:19–31)

READER 1 There was a rich man who was dressed in purple and fine linen and who feasted sumptuously every day. And at his gate lay a poor man named Lazarus, covered with sores, who longed to satisfy his hunger with what fell from the rich man's table; even the dogs would come and lick his sores.

READER 2 The poor man died and was carried away by the angels to be with Abraham. The rich man also died and was buried. In Hades, where he was being tormented, he looked up and saw Abraham far away with Lazarus by his side. He called out, "Father Abraham, have mercy on me, and send Lazarus to dip the tip of his finger in water and cool my tongue; for I am in agony in these flames."

READER 3 But Abraham said, "Child, remember that during your lifetime you received your good things, and Lazarus in like manner evil things; but now he is comforted here, and you are in agony. Besides all this, between you and us a great chasm has been fixed, so that those who might want to pass from here to you cannot do so, and no one can cross from there to us."

READER 4 He said, "Then, father, I beg you to send him to my father's house—for I have five brothers—that he may warn them, so that they will not also come into this place of torment."

READER 5 Abraham replied, "They have Moses and the prophets; they should listen to them." He said, "No, father Abraham; but if someone goes to them from the dead, they will repent."

READER 6 He said to him, "If they do not listen to Moses and the prophets, neither will they be convinced even if someone rises from the dead."

Reflection

LEADER Jesus often portrays the kingdom of God as a banquet. Using the banquet image, we see that the roles are reversed in the two banquet scenes—the first on earth and the second in heaven. In the first the poor man hoped for some bread on which the rich man wiped his hands. In the second we see the rich man hoping for some water from the poor man's fingertip. Satisfying hunger and thirst is within reach, but the only time such satisfaction can be achieved is on earth; it is too late in the afterlife.

Good deeds are always within reach. Ignoring the opportunities for good deeds can be a sin of omission. The rich man was not suffering punishment because of evil deeds like theft or murder; he just did not notice Lazarus. His indifference was his condemnation.

The opposite of love is not hate; it's indifference. If I hate someone, I'm still thinking of that person; if I'm indifferent, I don't give a thought to that person. Are there persons to whom I'm indifferent? How do I react to persons on the news who become homeless? What is my response when appeals for the needy are made? Do I pretend there are no problems in my school? Am I bothered enough to bother?

Do I believe that nothing can be changed? Do I believe I'm too powerless to bring about needed change? For what do I hope? How do I work to achieve my hopes? These hopes are a test of my Christianity, because Christian community in which no one is excluded is not just something to be achieved; it is the reality created by God in Christ in which we participate. The rich man would have been sitting at the heavenly banquet had he included the poor man.

Do we select where we will see Christ? Do we fail to share bread six days a week but come before God on Sunday asking for eucharistic bread? Such action seems incongruous. Service and liturgy go together. An early-third-century Syrian document states that charity is placed so completely at the heart of the liturgy that the bishop is told to sit on the floor and give up his throne to a poor man when he welcomes him into the gathering.

Activities (choose one)

1. Organize a project (leaf-raking, car wash, bake sale) to raise money for the needy in your town or state.

2. Ask local organizations who help the needy whether there are tasks students can perform.

3. Collect used stuffed animals, clean them, and give them to poor parishes for their festivals.

4. Ask persons from organizations like Catholic Charities or St. Vincent de Paul Society to speak to the class to dispel any myths you may have about the needy.

5. Pretend you are the rich man in the parable who is given another year of life to redeem himself. How would you spend the year? Does it resemble your life now?

6. Pretend Lazarus was permitted to visit the five brothers. Write a conversation between Lazarus raised from the dead and one brother.

Closing Prayer

LEADER   Let us pray.

ALL   Thank you, O God, for bothering about me when I don't take the time to bother about others who are your children.

LEADER   When I fail to help the needy, I fail you, O God. Yet you never fail me. When I've forgotten about the needy, you don't forget me in my need.

ALL   You are always there, always leading, surrounding me with your strength that I'm reluctant to share. Encourage me, invite me, to live your love.

LEADER   When I give to the needy, it is your love that is shared through mine.

ALL   When I feed the hungry and clothe the naked, I know that these actions will be rewarded with heaven, for you have said, "Come, blessed of my Father, for you gave food to the hungry." Amen.

Prayer Is the Only Way

Theme

Prayer increases our faith. Although prayer may seem impractical and useless, it is the only action that has real power to achieve God's plan.

Call to Prayer

LEADER   Loving God, we give to you our whole being. Please come to us in a closer way. Help us be open to whatever you ask us to be or do. Let us not hold anything back from you, but be willing to do whatever you want.

ALL   We surrender to you our family and friends, our health and talents, our success and limitations. We give you everything—our past, present, and future. We give you ourselves. We belong to you. If we have nothing but you, it is enough.

Reading (Luke 17:5–10)

READER 1   The apostles said to the Lord, "Increase our faith!"

READER 2   The Lord replied, "If you had faith the size of a mustard seed, you could say to this mulberry tree, 'Be uprooted and planted in the sea,' and it would obey you.

READER 3   "Who among you would say to your slave who has just come in from plowing or tending sheep in the field, 'Come here at once and take your place at the table'? Would you rather not say to him, 'Prepare supper for me, put on your apron and serve me while I eat and drink; later you may eat and drink'? Do you thank the slave for doing what was commanded? So you also, when you have done all that you were ordered to do, say, 'We are worthless slaves; we have done only what we ought to have done!'"

Reflection

LEADER   Faith is not coercing God into action. It is cooperating in God's activity in the world. To cooperate more with God's plan and to increase our faith, we need much prayer. Prayer increases our faith in a quiet but strong way. Prayer implies an attitude of letting go of our own plans and preferences and trying to see according to God's plan. This is why prayer increases our faith. But we would rather do things our own way and get rid of anything that we don't like. Getting rid of the problem seems a lot more practical and makes us feel a lot more secure than waiting upon God's way to reveal itself in prayer. Yet it is in the very waiting upon God, in the act of being vulnerable before God, in the silence of not knowing what to expect that our faith becomes powerful enough to move trees and much more. While it may seem at times that we're "only" praying and not doing very much, prayer is the only thing we can do. It's not a waste of time. Rather it's time "wasted on the Lord who never lets anything go to waste, but rather gathers our prayers like precious jewels."

This parable tells us that we Christians can never act as if we'd done enough for the kingdom. There is always something more that God needs accomplished through us. What are some of the things that need to be accomplished? Do we have faith that we will be able to have some impact on these needs?

How can we increase our faith?

Faith, hope, and love are called the theological virtues, because they come from God and take us to God. How does faith take us to God? Why is faith self-surrender to God and God's plan?

Faith is certain. What makes it certain? Faith can be tested. How do we pass the test of faith?

Activities (choose one)

1. If there is a great problem in your school or town, decide to form a group to pray together once a week about this problem. Decide upon a time, place, and type of prayer. Throughout the week continue to pray for this problem individually, and do some fasting. Pray until the problem is gone, and then continue to pray in thanksgiving for some additional weeks.

2. Decide upon doing something extra for God; for example, give money to a good cause, spend 10–15 minutes a day reading Scripture, visit the sick, or involve yourself in a project to help the needy. Ask God for the faith that you will not miss the lost time and that you will have time for everything else you need besides. Do this for as many weeks as you can.

3. Write the word "faith" vertically. Surround each letter with other letters to spell five words that relate to faith. Possibly shape the words into a diamond by making the longest word the middle word. Then below the diamond, write a sentence beginning, "Faith is like a diamond, because..."

Closing Prayer

LEADER O God, we have come before you in faith. We have trusted that your Word is true.

SIDE 1 Thank you for sending us the Holy Spirit to teach us and help us pray. Thank you for the Spirit's gifts of faith, hope, and love.

SIDE 2   Thank you for loving each of us unconditionally. Thank you for being there in every moment of our lives. Thank you for lifting us when we fall and for carrying us over the rough places.

SIDE 1   Thank you for letting us be part of your plan for the world and helping you bring about the fullness of the kingdom.

SIDE 2   Thank you for all the blessings of our lives, especially our family, friends, and those who have helped us.

ALL   Thank you for the gift of life. Above all, thank you for the gift of your Son Jesus, in whom we place all our faith. Amen.

Grateful Hearts Are Happy Hearts

Theme

The secret of being happy is a grateful heart.

Materials Needed

Stories of modern-day miracles, paper, chalk, cassette tape of a song of praise and thanksgiving

Call to Prayer

LEADER   O God, we cannot praise you enough. To you alone belongs the glory!

ALL   "It is good to give thanks to the Lord, to sing praises to your name, O Most High; to declare your steadfast love in the morning, and your faithfulness by night."
(Play a song of praise and thanksgiving. Example: Jim Cowan)

Reading (Luke 17:11–19)

READER 1   On the way to Jerusalem Jesus was going through the region between Samaria and Galilee. As he entered a village, ten lepers approached him. Keeping their distance, they called out, saying, "Jesus, Master, have mercy on us!"

READER 2   When he saw them, he said to them, "Go and show yourselves to the priests." And as they went, they were made clean.

READER 3   Then one of them, when he saw that he was healed, turned back, praising God with a loud voice. He prostrated himself at Jesus' feet and thanked him. And he was a Samaritan. Then Jesus asked, "Were not ten made clean? But the other nine, where are they? Was none of them found to return and give praise to God except this foreigner?"

READER 4   Then he said to him, "Get up and go on your way; your faith has made you well."

Reflection

LEADER The Samaritan leper knew the secret of being happy: it is to be grateful. His praise of God in a loud voice was a sacrifice of praise. His grateful heart is an example for us.

Are we grateful persons? Do we moan about what we don't possess more than we thank God for what we do have? Is our happiness dependent upon the number and quality of things that we own?

The grateful ex-leper may not have been a welcome example to the listeners in Jesus' day. No one expected a Samaritan leper to do anything good, even as they never expected the Good Samaritan of another Gospel story to bind an injured person's wounds. God's People, then and now, do not have a monopoly on goodness. Goodness must be appreciated in every person.

Are there certain persons or groups of people that we expect to be less good? Are there certain persons or groups that we expect to be very good? What impact do such expectations have on these persons?

Activities (choose one)

1. Divide the chalkboard into twelve parts for the months of the year, and divide the class into twelve groups, one for each month. Make a mural about events for which you are grateful in those months.

2. Give each student a letter of the alphabet. Make a list of persons, places, and things for which you are grateful that begin with that particular letter. Pray these together, starting with A. These could be written on papers and made into a booklet of prayer starters titled "Thanking God from A to Z."

3. Discuss how persons become what we expect them to be. Research lives of persons who overcame tremendous odds, because one person believed in them. Share these biographical sketches in short speeches, or write these anecdotes on hearts. Place them on a bulletin board with the caption "Grateful Hearts Are Happy Hearts."

Closing Prayer

LEADER Thank you, God, for your continual presence in our lives.

SIDE 1 Thank you, God, for the beauty of creation and your beautiful children.

SIDE 2 Thank you, God, for persons who believe in us and help us be the best we can be.

SIDE 1 Thank you, God, for miracles of health, new life, and happiness.

SIDE 2 Thank you, God, for this class, for learning and growing, for deepening our faith.

SIDE 1 Thank you, God, for your Word that guides us and your Sacrament that nourishes us.

SIDE 2 Thank you, God, for transforming us into the Body of Christ. Thank you for the privilege of being your hands, feet, and voice in our world.

SIDE 1 Thank you, for preserving us from sin and giving us the strength to do the right thing.

SIDE 2 Thank you, O God, for letting us meet you along the way and be open to your power to heal us of the ills of body and soul.

ALL Let us always return to you to give thanks. Amen.

Keep On Praying

Theme

We may never stop praying. When God doesn't seem to answer our prayer, we keep asking and trusting.

Materials Needed

Photos of persons praying

Call to Prayer

LEADER Lord Jesus Christ, pray for us as our priest, pray in us as our Head, and hear our prayers as our God. We gratefully acknowledge your praying in us and our praying in you.

ALL Lord Jesus Christ, may your prayer to your Father be a model of our prayer. May your solitude in early morning and in deserted spaces be our guide to learning prayer. May your confidence in prayer be our own, even when the prayer seems unheard, as you yourself experienced in the agony in the garden and on the cross.

Reading (Luke 18:1–8)

READER 1 Then Jesus told them a parable about their need to pray always and not to lose heart.

READER 2 He said, "In a certain city there was a judge who neither feared God nor had respect for people. In that city there was a widow who kept coming to him and saying, 'Grant me justice against my opponent.'

READER 3 "For a while he refused, but later he said to himself, 'Though I have no fear of God and no respect for anyone, yet because this widow keeps bothering me, I will grant her justice, so that she may not wear me out by continually coming.'"

READER 4 And the Lord said, "Listen to what the unjust judge says. And will not God grant justice to his chosen ones who cry to him day and night? Will he delay long in helping them? I tell you, he will quickly grant justice to them. And yet, when the Son of Man comes, will he find faith on earth?"

Reflection

LEADER   Have you ever prayed for something for a very long time and it seemed as if God would never answer? Are you praying in that way now for something important to you? What does it feel like when God seems to have a deaf ear? Does it make you want to stop praying? Does God's silence make you feel that you are asking for the wrong thing? Do you say, "Well, I prayed for three months, so I'm going to quit praying"?

Praying for a week or two may make us feel good about ourselves. Praying for a month may get tedious or even boring. Praying for a half-year may seem foolish. But praying for a year or more has the potential to let us know God in a very intimate way.

When we sustain our faith-filled prayer over a very long time, we become our prayer. We no longer just say prayers, but are transformed into a prayer-filled person. We understand what it means to pray always and not lose heart. And this constant prayer for one cause profoundly impacts all our other prayers. In every prayer we find ourselves more open to God and the words of Scripture, and we find new depths in ourselves. Maybe we discover new gifts of the Spirit that have been released in us through the constant prayer. At the very least we begin to understand God's timelessness, as we trust that God "will quickly grant justice."

How would you describe prayer done in faith? How would you describe prayer done in filial boldness? How would you describe prayer done in watchfulness? How would you describe prayer done in patience?

Activities (choose one)

1. Using a Concordance, find many examples of prayer in the New Testament. What do these examples teach us about prayer?

2. Design a page for a yearbook titled "Praying with Passion" that tells about qualities of prayer and shows photos of students praying.

3. As a class, choose one local concern needing prayer. Pray for that concern every time your class meets.

4. We sometimes speak of four types of prayer whose first letters spell "pact": petition, adoration, contrition, and thanksgiving. In groups, write one-line prayers of each type. Put these on cards that can be used personally. Make a pact with God to pray these four types of prayer daily.

Closing Prayer

LEADER   We bless you, O God, for you are the source of every blessing.

ALL   We adore you, O God, for your greatness and creativity.

LEADER   We ask forgiveness, O God, for the times we chose deeds contrary to gospel values.

ALL We thank you, O God, for the gift of life, for our family and friends, for parties and good times, for success and happiness, for every good gift with which you have blessed us.

LEADER We petition you, O God, for the needs we now present.
(Spontaneous petitions)

LEADER Keep us faithful to prayer all the days of our lives. Put a prayer in our heart for every step of our journey to you. May we never cease praying, because you never cease loving us and wanting to give us everything we need.

ALL Amen.

Trusting God More than Yourself

Theme

Looking at God gives us better perspective about ourselves.

Call to Prayer

LEADER   O God, help us come before you to pray with a proper attitude.

ALL   We wish to be humble before you, acknowledging your greatness. Yet at the same time we are confident of your care and generous blessing.

LEADER   Help us now and always not to spend times of prayer talking to ourselves rather than to you, or listing our qualities as if we had to prove ourselves. But rather let us concentrate on you.

ALL   Make us willing even to remain silent in your presence.

Reading (Luke 18:9–14)

READER 1   Jesus also told this parable to some who trusted in themselves that they were righteous and regarded others with contempt:

READER 2   "Two men went up to the temple to pray, one a Pharisee and the other a tax collector. The Pharisee, standing by himself, was praying thus, 'God, I thank you that I am not like other people: thieves, rogues, adulterers, or even like this tax collector. I fast twice a week; I give a tenth of all my income.'

READER 3   "But the tax collector, standing far off, would not even look up to heaven, but was beating his breast and saying, 'God, be merciful to me, a sinner!'

READER 4   "I tell you, this man went down to his home justified rather than the other; for all who exalt themselves will be humbled, but all who humble themselves will be exalted."

Reflection

LEADER   The Pharisee's big mistake was that he didn't trust God to know his deeds, so he went to the Temple to inform God of his goodness. We can imagine him saying, "God, I wanted to let you know that I abstained even from water Monday and Thursday." The publican's big advantage, on the other hand, was that he trusted God more than himself. He acknowledged God as supremely merciful. When we trust God more than ourselves, that is our greatness. When we accept humbly God's greatness, then we are exalted.

When might teens hold others in contempt as the Pharisee held the publican in contempt? How does one overcome contempt so that people are not seen as inferior?

When things are going badly, we need to trust God's merciful love. How does God show merciful love?

Activities (choose one)

1. Dramatize this parable as it is, or make it a present-day version applicable to the local or national scene. How does it feel to be the downtrodden person who ultimately will be exalted? How does it feel to be the highly respected person who ultimately will be brought low?

2. Write a resume for being a liturgical minister, such as lector, cantor, presider, or eucharistic minister. Emphasize qualities that show that although you have talents and skills, you know that in church ministry God's power is more important than personal abilities.

Closing Prayer

LEADER   God, when I feel like a failure, you are there for me.

ALL   When I am successful, you are again there.

LEADER   When I am filled with complaints, you are listening.

ALL   When I am filled with gratitude, you are receiving my thanks.

LEADER   When my faith fails me, you are there to assure me.

ALL   When I trust your help, you are giving support.

LEADER   When I feel boastful and proud, you remind me that all comes from you.

ALL   When I feel humiliated, you raise me out of my shame.

LEADER   When I am too ashamed to raise my eyes to heaven, you are beside me to say everything will be all right.

ALL   When I know that my heart is true to you, it is a reflection of your own belief in me. Amen.

Saints Are on Christ's Team

Theme

The saints of heaven and the saints of earth form one team to fulfill God's "game plan." As a good team, the saints have the same motivation, namely, love.

Materials Needed

Items to make a game board

Call to Prayer

LEADER   With all the saints—those on the church calendar and those we hold dear in our hearts—let us praise God.

ALL   "Amen! Blessing and glory and wisdom and thanksgiving and honor and power and might be to our God forever and ever! Amen!" (Rev 7:12)

Reading (Matthew 5:1–12)

READER 1   When Jesus saw the crowds, he went up the mountain; and after he sat down, his disciples came to him. Then he began to speak, and taught them, saying:

READER 2   "Blessed are the poor in spirit, for theirs is the kingdom of heaven.

READER 3   "Blessed are those who mourn, for they will be comforted.

READER 4   "Blessed are the meek, for they will inherit the earth.

READER 5   "Blessed are those who hunger and thirst for righteousness, for they will be filled.

READER 6   "Blessed are the merciful, for they will receive mercy.

READER 7   "Blessed are the pure in heart, for they will see God.

READER 8   "Blessed are the peacemakers, for they will be called children of God.

READER 9   "Blessed are those who are persecuted for righteousness' sake, for theirs is the kingdom of heaven.

READER 10 "Blessed are you when people revile you and persecute you and utter all kinds of evil against you falsely on my account. Rejoice and be glad, for your reward is great in heaven, for in the same way they persecuted the prophets who were before you."

Reflection

LEADER As Christians we are never alone. We are an integral part of one another, just as hands and feet are integral to the body. What binds us together is the love of God whose Trinitarian love is the perfection of community. Father, Son, and Holy Spirit love each other perfectly, communicate perfectly, and have the same eagerness to share themselves with us.

The saints in heaven participate in this stupendous love, and we (saints-in-the-making) also participate in God's love through grace. The way we become saints is to become a team of love right here on earth. The love of heaven and earth combine in One Love, who is God. All Saints Day is the time to remember that we're on the same team as our relatives and friends who have gone before us. We're all in this together.

What does God's Team of Love need to achieve? What "game plan" can the team on earth use to achieve the goal? How can the saints of heaven and saints on earth work together?

Because the beatitudes are ways that Christ has given us to achieve the "game plan" of salvation, list some practical ways to accomplish each; for example, how can we be pure of heart, merciful, and happy despite persecution?

Activities (choose one)

1. Choose a sport such as football, soccer, or cross country. Using the terminology and players of that sport, explain how God, the saints in heaven, and the saints on earth can achieve bringing all people into salvation, that is, into the circle of God's redeeming love. (The whole class could choose one sport, or several groups could choose different sports.)

2. Create a board game called "Saints," "God's Team," or "Kingdom" for younger students. The aim of the game is to have the saints on earth and the saints in heaven achieve the same goal.

Closing Prayer

LEADER Let us pray a short litany of saints to ask their help that we may continue the work they have begun.

SIDE 1 Holy Mary, Mother of God and of the church, help us be as attentive to God's Word as you were.

SIDE 2 Holy Angels of God, who continually adore God, help us put God first in our lives.

SIDE 1	Saint Joseph, patron of the dying, give blessings to all who are sick and dying.
SIDE 2	Holy Apostles, upon whom the church is built, help us "make church" by being involved in our parishes.
SIDE 1	Saint John the Baptist, who pointed the way to Jesus, make us signs that point to God.
SIDE 2	Saint Mary Magdalene, who proclaimed the resurrection, help us believe that good follows suffering.
SIDE 1	Saint Stephen, martyred for your belief and preaching, make us fearless when we need to stand up for our values and beliefs.
SIDE 2	Saint Teresa of Avila and Saint Thérèse of Lisieux, whose love of the church gave you the title "doctor," make us holy members of the church.
SIDE 1	Saint Elizabeth, who knew even the hidden presence of Christ, help us see Christ when he is hidden in unlikely persons and situations.
SIDE 2	Saint Martha, who worked hard in humble ways to serve the Lord, help us work hard at home to serve Christ in our family.
SIDE 1	Saint Maximilian Kolbe, priest who died in a concentration camp to save the life of another, give us courage to sacrifice so that others may survive.
SIDE 2	Saint Elizabeth Seton, first native-born saint from the United States, and pioneer in religious education, help all teachers and students learn more about Christ.
SIDE 1	All holy men and women, pray for us.
SIDE 2	All parents and grandparents, friends and relatives who see the Lord face to face, bring us one day to that same glory.
LEADER	May we be your saints too in all that we say and in all that we do. Continue your work in us and may all your saints in heaven guide us.
ALL	Amen.

Free At Last!

Theme

To become fully human we need to be free.

Materials Needed

Paper, pencils

Call to Prayer

LEADER   O God, whose love is unconditional, we come before you to give to you anything in our life that is holding us back from being the best we can be.

ALL   We give you our fears and worries, our addictions and bad habits, our grief and our longings. Help us release our weaknesses so that our true character may surface. Keep us focused on you. We believe you can free us from anything holding us back from your love. And we ask you to let us go free.

Reading (Luke 19:1–10)

READER 1   Jesus entered Jericho and was passing through it. A man was there named Zacchaeus; he was a chief tax collector and was rich. He was trying to see who Jesus was, but on account of the crowd he could not, because he was short in stature. So he ran ahead and climbed a sycamore tree to see him, because he was going to pass that way.

READER 2   When Jesus came to the place, he looked up and said to him, "Zacchaeus, hurry and come down; for I must stay at your house today." So he hurried down and was happy to welcome him. All who saw it began to grumble and said, "He has gone to be the guest of one who is a sinner."

READER 3   Zacchaeus stood there and said to the Lord, "Look, half of my possessions, Lord, I will give to the poor; and if I have defrauded anyone of anything, I will pay back four times as much."

READER 4   Then Jesus said to him, "Today salvation has come to this house, because he too is a son of Abraham. For the Son of Man came to seek out and to save the lost."

Reflection

LEADER   Salvation came to Zacchaeus when he was freed of his addiction to money.

Jesus liberated him so that he could become who he was meant to be. It has been suggested that all of us are addicted to something. It may not be a strong addiction or even a bad one, but the attraction can prevent us from being our best selves. Freedom is the foundation for becoming the person God intends us to be.

What may be some addictions common to teens? How can teens become freed of these addictions?

Jesus searched out Zacchaeus. When Jesus searches for us, do we want to be found? Would we rather remain "lost"?

Leo Tolstoy said, "Everybody thinks of changing humanity and nobody thinks of changing himself." When Zacchaeus changed himself, do you think this change had any effect on others?

Activities (choose one)

1. Work on one addiction this week; for example, forgo a favorite television show, play games on the computer less frequently, give up surfing the Internet, spend less time on the phone, or sacrifice certain foods.

2. Draw a stick figure of yourself chained to a stake. On the links of the chain write those things that prevent you from being the best you can be. Near the chain write those things that would free you from your bondage.

3. What has you "up a tree"? Draw yourself in a tree and imagine what hope you are placing in Jesus. When Jesus stops by your tree, what favor will you ask him? Write the dialogue between you and Jesus in comic strip form.

Closing Prayer

LEADER   Let us pray an act of contrition.

ALL   Merciful God, forgive us for the times we strayed from you to choose greed or pride or laziness rather than your love.

LEADER   For the times we thought we could get along without you, we are sorry.

ALL   For the times we forgot that you were present in all we met, we are sorry.

LEADER   For the times we were selfish with money, time, and talents, we are sorry.

ALL   For letting our addictions become stronger, we are sorry. Forgive us, Lord. Come to our house, dine with us, and change us forever. Amen.

Morality Is an Inside Job

Theme

Although moral decisions are based on objective laws, morality comes from within. Morality is being who we are in Christ.

Materials Needed

Mirrors, markers, Bibles

Call to Prayer

LEADER Heavenly Father, we your children come before you to ask you to help us become the kind of people you want us to be.

ALL O God, you have a picture of us, and you see us as very beautiful, even though we don't see ourselves that way.

LEADER You know what kind of people we are and who we want to become, even better than we can ever imagine.

ALL Give us the courage to answer the question, "What kind of person do I want to become?" And give us the courage and wisdom to know that who we are meant to be is your wonderful image of us.

LEADER Help us become who we are in Christ.

Reading (Luke 20:27–38)

READER 1 Some Sadducees, those who say there is no resurrection, came to him and asked him a question, "Teacher, Moses wrote for us that if a man's brother dies, leaving a wife but no children, the man shall marry the widow and raise up children for his brother. Now there were seven brothers; the first married, and died childless; then the second and the third married her, and so in the same way all seven died childless. Finally the woman also died. In the resurrection, therefore, whose wife will the woman be? For the seven had married her."

READER 2 Jesus said to them, "Those who belong to this age marry and are given in marriage; but those who are considered worthy of a place in that age and in the resurrection from the dead neither marry nor are given in marriage. Indeed they cannot die anymore, because they are like angels and are children of God, being children of the resurrection. And the fact that the dead are raised Moses himself showed, in the story about the bush, where he speaks of the Lord as the God of Abraham, the God of Isaac, and the God of Jacob. Now he is God not of the dead but of the living; for to him all of them are alive."

Reflection

LEADER   Jesus' morality was quite different from that of the Sadducees. While the Sadducees looked to Jewish Law, Jesus looked within himself to find his Father's will. Like Jesus, we need to ask, "God, what do you want me to do?" As we make moral decisions, we look deep within ourselves where God resides. This does not mean we ignore objective norms and laws like the Ten Commandments, the Beatitudes, church laws, civil laws, school handbooks, or parental guidelines. No, most of our decisions will be based on these laws; however, there may be situations that require deeper thinking and creative solutions that words on a page cannot give. Just as Jesus came with a fresh solution to the problem of who's married to whom in heaven, we need to mature in creative responses that solve our problems best.

In this particular gospel passage, Jesus sees a deeper question; namely, "Who is God?" His answer is clear: God is a God of the living. Once we know who God is, then moral decision making becomes bigger than looking at laws; morality becomes looking at God and looking at who we are and trying to become the best image of God that we can be. Morality is becoming who we are. Evelyn Underhill said, "A saint is a human being who has become a pure capacity for God, and therefore a tool of the divine action." How do we become more saintly, more like God, more fully human, more who we are meant to be in Christ?

When we are more like Christ, more like the image God has of us, how does that affect our moral decision making?

Activities (choose one)

1. Read the Scripture passages listed below. Then in one word or short phrase describe Jesus in that passage. If that word or phrase described you, how would that affect your moral decision making?

The Temptation of Jesus (Mt 4:1–11), New Law of Retaliation (Mt 5:38–42), Love of Enemies (Mt 5:43–47), Cure of Peter's Mother-in-Law (Mt 8:14–15), Call of Matthew (Mt 9:9–13), Mission of the Twelve (Mt 9:35–38), Cure of the Man with a Shriveled Hand (Mt 12:9–15)

2. Write on a mirror words that characterize Jesus Christ. Spend some moments looking into the mirror to see whether you can see yourself in those characteristics. Use one mirror for the whole class, or divide into groups for this task.

Closing Prayer

LEADER   Loving God, when I feel that I am not worth much,

ALL   help me remember that I am made in your image.

LEADER   When I am afraid of making mistakes,

ALL   help me realize mistakes can help me learn.

LEADER   When I stay with the safe, the known, the tried-and-true,

ALL   give me the courage to explore new opportunities and interests in order to grow.

LEADER   When I act superior or inferior to others,

ALL   help me be happy with myself.

LEADER   When I am defensive toward criticism,

ALL   let me see in criticism a potential means for maturing.

LEADER   When I look into the mirror and see only myself,

ALL   let me see your image and remember that my best self is who I am in Christ.

LEADER   When I make moral decisions,

ALL   guide me with your Spirit to choose according to the example of Jesus Christ. Amen.

What Christ Was and Did We Are Meant to Be and Do

Theme

Salvation history is never finished; it continues in us. Persons in every age participate in a process of becoming like Christ. Our responsibility in the new millennium is to be and do what Christ was and did.

Materials Needed

Bibles, research materials describing Christians in the first two millennia (approximately 30 C.E.–1000 C.E and 1000 C.E.–2000 C.E.)

Call to Prayer

LEADER   O God, when we fear the future, we come to you to find safety and protection.

ALL   Be our rock of refuge, a stronghold that gives us safety. Bring light and joy into the darkness of this world.

LEADER   Give hope to the despairing and joy to the sorrowing.

ALL   Give justice to the oppressed and freedom to those unjustly imprisoned. Give health and strength to the sick and wisdom to those making decisions.

LEADER   When we search for you because we don't know what to do, reveal yourself to us. When we fear the future, remind us that you hold the future in your hands.

ALL   We praise and adore you, the God who is, who was, and who is to come.

Reading (Luke 21:5–19)

READER 1   When some were speaking about the temple, how it was adorned with beautiful stones and gifts dedicated to God, he said, "As for these things that you see, the days will come when not one stone will be left upon another; all will be thrown down."

READER 2   They asked him, "Teacher, when will this be, and what will be the sign that this is about to take place?"

READER 3   And he said, "Beware that you are not led astray; for many will come in my name and say, 'I am he!' and, 'The time is near!' Do not go after them.

READER 4   "When you hear of wars and insurrections, do not be terrified; for these things must take place first, but the end will not follow immediately."

READER 5   Then he said to them, "Nation will rise against nation, and kingdom against kingdom; there will be great earthquakes, and in various places famines and plagues; and there will be dreadful portents and great signs from heaven.

READER 6   "But before all this occurs, they will arrest you and persecute you; they will hand you over to synagogues and prisons, and you will be brought before kings and governors because of my name. This will give you an opportunity to testify.

READER 7   "So make up your minds not to prepare your defense in advance; for I will give you words and a wisdom that none of your opponents will be able to withstand or contradict. You will be betrayed even by parents and brothers, by relatives and friends; and they will put some of you to death. You will be hated by all because of my name. But not a hair of your head will perish. By your endurance you will gain your souls."

Reflection

LEADER   Luke teaches that Christians must adjust to a long period of waiting, including persecution. In this they are following the crucified Christ, who arrived at glory after great endurance. Every gospel account has this same truth: what Christ did and was, we too must do and be in him. For this reason salvation history is never finished; it continues in us until the Second Coming. Ultimately God will be completely glorified and we in him. Christ saves in every age, and we have saints from every century to prove it. Even now we are in the process of conversion, of becoming saints, and are constantly becoming who we are meant to be. Christ's story is our story: he overcame adversity, even death; and so will we.

The new millennium forces us to look at the future. Will Christ come in the new millennium in all his glory? Whether tomorrow or another millennium away, our role is to become what baptism initiated in us: children of God, members of the kingdom, prophets and priests. How can you best be a child of God this week?

How does being a member of the kingdom now and in the future affect the decisions you make and the actions you make today? In what ways are you a prophet? What is your priestly role in the church? How do you feel being a young person at the beginning of a new millennium? What is your responsibility?

Activities (choose one)

1. What Christ did and was we are meant to do and be. Divide the class into four groups, one for each gospel. Page through the gospel, stopping at places that help paint a portrait of who Jesus was and what he was. After listing several characteristics of Jesus, write how you can live these characteristics, too. Don't forget to include the ordinary things of life like feeding the dog, washing the car, mowing the lawn, as well as some specifically religious things like serving or reading at Mass or performing acts of kindness.

2. Briefly research what Christianity was like in the first millennium and in the second millennium. What would you like to see in Christians during the third millennium?

3. We want to be ready whenever Jesus comes in glory. Religion is real when it affects our everyday experiences. Describe a typical day in the life of a teen. What choices would teens make if they realized the Second Coming would be that day?

Closing Prayer

LEADER   Christ, you are Lord of the cosmos and of history.

SIDE 1   Christ, you are head of the church, which is your Body.

SIDE 2   Christ, you have taught us that we are already in the "last hour," the renewal of the world, the final age.

SIDE 1   Fulfill your reign in glory by returning to the earth.

SIDE 2   Bring everything under your kingship, establish fully your messianic kingdom, and preserve your church from trials and persecutions that may shake our faith. Fulfill the victory over sin already accomplished in your death and resurrection.

ALL   Come, Lord Jesus, come! Reign over us now and in the age to come. Amen.

God's Reign Is One of Mercy, Compassion, and Equality

Theme

Christ's reign is one of mercy, compassion, and equality.

Materials Needed

Art materials in the seven colors of the rainbow

Call to Prayer

LEADER   Let us pray Psalm 93 praising the majesty of God's rule.

SIDE 1   The Lord is king; he is robed in majesty;

SIDE 2   the Lord is robed, he is girded with strength.

SIDE 1   He has established the world; it shall never be moved;

SIDE 2   your throne is established from of old; you are from everlasting.

SIDE 1   The floods have lifted up, O Lord, the floods have lifted up their voice; the floods lift up their roaring.

SIDE 2   More majestic than the thunders of mighty waters, more majestic than the waves of the sea, majestic on high is the Lord!

ALL   Your decrees are very sure; holiness befits your house, O Lord, forevermore.

Reading (Luke 23:35–43)

READER 1   The people stood by, watching; but the leaders scoffed at Jesus, saying, "He saved others; let him save himself if he is the Messiah of God, his chosen one!"

READER 2   The soldiers also mocked him, coming up and offering him sour wine, and saying, "If you are the King of the Jews, save yourself!" There was also an inscription over him, "This is the King of the Jews."

READER 3   One of the criminals who was hanged there kept deriding him and saying, "Are you not the Messiah? Save yourself and us!"

READER 4   But the other rebuked him, saying, "Do you not fear God since you are under the same sentence of condemnation? And we indeed have been condemned justly, for we are getting what we deserve for our deeds, but this man has done nothing wrong."

READER 5   Then he said, "Jesus, remember me when you come into your kingdom." He replied, "Truly I tell you, today you will be with me in Paradise."

Reflection

LEADER   Publicans, tax collectors, sinners of all kinds were counted among Jesus' friends in life. Now in death Jesus' first act as king is an executive pardon to a criminal. "Today you will be with me in Paradise" is the assurance that social privilege, economic status, religious background have no bearing on who's who in the kingdom. Such a reversal of earthly values proves that the reign of God will be one of mercy, compassion, and equality.

What kinds of people do you expect to find in the kingdom of God? What kinds of people would you be surprised to find in heaven? What do these two answers say about ourselves?

Every time we gather for liturgy (whether Eucharist, other sacraments, or Liturgy of the Hours), we are involved in resisting hopelessness, a feeling of no future, and disappointment in an unjust world. Liturgy is an act of worship that gives us complete hope, a sense of future, and trust in each other. How does liturgy achieve this?

The reign of God began with the death-resurrection of Jesus and continues today, reaching its fullness in the final age. As we strive to bring about the fullness of the reign of God, how can we show a reign of compassion? of forgiveness and mercy? of equality?

Activities (choose one)

1. Illustrate the kingdom of God as a rainbow. What do the seven colors represent?

2. Thanksgiving Day occurs near the Feast of Christ the King. Write a letter of gratitude to someone who has influenced you to be a better person.

3. Christ the King rules over all creation for the Father "has put all things under his feet" (see Eph 1:20–22). Write a litany of thanksgiving for the gifts of creation. Sample: Christ, King of the Universe, thank you for the sun, stars, and planets. Christ, King of the World, thank you for mountains and streams. Christ, King of our hearts, thank you for teaching us love.

Closing Prayer

LEADER   Christ, King of mercy and compassion, make us a people of mercy and compassion.

SIDE 1   Open our eyes to the needs of others so that our good deeds may be worthy of the kingdom.

SIDE 2   Open our ears and our mouths to the song of the universe, the hymn of praise from all creation, that we may be worthy to join the song.

SIDE 1   Open our hearts to each and every person who is part of the kingdom, that we may be worthy to enjoy eternity with them.

SIDE 2   Open our hands in welcome so that no one is excluded from the kingdom.

ALL   May our good deeds merit for us the words, "Come into the kingdom prepared for you." Amen.

Patterning Our Lives on Christ's

Theme

The purpose of the church year is to fill up what is lacking in us until we pattern our lives fully on Christ.

Materials Needed

Stencils, paint, and heavy paper or tagboard to make Christmas cards; video of *Martin the Cobbler*

Call to Prayer

LEADER   As Advent begins we as church reread and relive the great events of salvation.

SIDE 1   Lord Jesus Christ, who came once long ago in Bethlehem, who comes today into our lives, and who will come again in glory, be with us this Advent to await your coming.

SIDE 2   Patterning our lives on you, Lord Jesus, may we too be in a process of coming: coming into maturity, coming to serve, coming to bring comfort, and coming like Advent candles to light people's lives with the glow of Christ's light.

Reading (Matthew 24:37–44)

READER 1   For as the days of Noah were, so will be the coming of the Son of Man. For as in those days before the flood they were eating and drinking, marrying and giving in marriage, until the day Noah entered the ark, and they knew nothing until the flood came and swept them all away, so too will be the coming of the Son of Man.

READER 2   Then two will be in the field; one will be taken and one will be left. Two women will be grinding meal together; one will be taken and one will be left.

READER 3   Keep awake therefore, for you do not know on what day your Lord is coming. But understand this: if the owner of the house had known in what part of the night the thief was coming, he would have stayed awake and would not have let his house be broken into. Therefore you also must be ready, for the Son of Man is coming at an unexpected hour.

Reflection

LEADER   The church year helps us fill up what is lacking in us until we, the church, can pattern our lives fully on Christ. No church year is like any other. Every Advent, for example, we are one year closer to the Parousia or Second Coming. We don't just go around a liturgical circle and come back to the same starting point; rather we live the church year as if it were a spiral, each year getting closer to the goal of patterning our lives fully on Christ.

How are you more like Christ this year than last year? What events of the past year will help you appreciate Christmas more?

The people in the gospel story were not sinning; they were simply preoccupied with their duty and occupation and gave no thought to impending catastrophe. What occupies our thoughts most often? Do we take the time to think about spiritual things like growing in character and listening to God to know God's will? If we were to pattern our thoughts on the thoughts of Christ, what words would describe our thoughts? If you knew Jesus were coming next week, how would you spend this week?

Activities (choose one)

1. Make Christmas cards for the homebound or residents in nursing homes. Use a stencil and write the words "Pattern your life on Jesus, the Gift."

2. List as many things that you did today as you can recall. Then contemplate the possibility of Jesus coming tomorrow. Cross off your list anything you wish you had not done, and add to your list what you feel you need to accomplish before tomorrow.

3. View *Martin the Cobbler* or read the story by Leo Tolstoy on which it is based. What is its message about the coming of Christ?

Closing Prayer

LEADER   After each statement, please respond "May we pattern our lives on Christ's."

Christ came as "love following upon love" to teach us the way of love. (Response.)

Christ came to bring hope to a darkened world. (Response.)

Christ came to teach us to serve and not be served. (Response.)

Christ came to heal the world of division and hatred. (Response.)

Christ came to heal pain and suffering. (Response.)

ALL   Christ, when you come again in glory, see that we have filled up what is lacking in us so that we can be perfectly identified with you. Amen.

Hurry!
The Kingdom Is Here!

Theme

Although we await the Parousia, salvation is here in Christ, and sacred history continues in us.

Materials Needed

Art materials to make a Christmas card

Call to Prayer

LEADER Lord, during the second week of Advent, help us continue to make the path straight and smooth for your coming. Where there is the wilderness of confusion,

ALL let us bring wise judgment and right thinking.

LEADER Where there are high mountains of egotism and elitism,

ALL let us bring humility.

LEADER Where there are valleys of despair and anxiety,

ALL let us bring hope and peace.

Reading (Matthew 3:1–12)

READER 1 In those days John the Baptist appeared in the wilderness of Judea, proclaiming, "Repent, for the kingdom of heaven has come near."

READER 2 This is the one of whom the prophet Isaiah spoke when he said, "The voice of one crying out in the wilderness: 'Prepare the way of the Lord, make his paths straight.'"

READER 3 Now John wore clothing of camel's hair with a leather belt around his waist, and his food was locusts and wild honey. Then the people of Jerusalem and all Judea were going out to him, and all the region along the Jordan, and they were baptized by him in the river Jordan, confessing their sins.

READER 4 But when he saw many Pharisees and Sadducees coming for baptism, he said to them, "You brood of vipers! Who warned you to flee from the wrath to come? Bear fruit worthy of repentance. Do not presume to say to yourselves, 'We have Abraham as our ancestor'; for I tell you, God is able from these stones to raise up children to Abraham. Even now the axe is lying at the root of the trees; every tree therefore that does not bear good fruit is cut down and thrown into the fire.

READER 5 "I baptize you with water for repentance, but one who is more powerful than I is coming after me; I am not worthy to carry his sandals. He will baptize you with the Holy Spirit and fire. His winnowing fork is in his hand, and he will clear his threshing floor and will gather his wheat into the granary; but the chaff he will burn with unquenchable fire."

Reflection

LEADER John the Baptist claims that salvation is here in the person of Jesus Christ. Salvation history is "personalized" in him. We, his followers, no longer await salvation; it is here, and it continues in us. Bear good fruit now. Get rid of the chaff now. There's immediacy in John the Baptist's voice, because the axe is at the root right now. "Don't be complacent," John seems to say. Nothing can wait. The kingdom of God is at hand.

How do we bring salvation to our world today? What can we do about AIDS, drugs, drive-by shootings, fraud, vandalism, and missing persons? How can we bring salvation to this classroom? to our families? to our neighborhoods? In what ways does salvation history continue in us? What are qualifications to get into the kingdom? In what sense could we say that only "nobodies" are qualified?

Activity

This time of year can be very pretty: snow on evergreens, colorful lights, breathtaking decorations, precious scenes of children. But Christmas is more than a warm glow. John the Baptist reminds us that God entered our world to rid it of sin. Christ came as light into darkness, as goodness into evil, as one who conquers death and sin by shedding blood in the midst of raging evil. Make a Christmas card that would appeal to John the Baptist. Use one of the following as a theme: (a) we continue salvation history in the wilderness of our present world, (b) Christ came as light into darkness, (c) the Messiah came to die for sin.

Closing Prayer

LEADER Saint John the Baptist, herald of the good news of Christ's coming, help us be prophets leading to salvation.

ALL Help us speak out against injustice, righting wrongs through peace and good will.

Help us continue the work of Christ who conquered sin.

Help us bear good fruit in acts of service and generosity.

Help us avoid the complacency that says we have plenty of time to reform our lives.

Help us bring about the kingdom in our homes and schools.

Help us to hurry, for the kingdom of God is at hand. Amen.

Union with God: the Best Christmas Gift

Theme

God became human, so we could become like God. God became a child, so we could be called "children of God." Our union with God is a powerful reality.

Materials Needed

Christmas carols and Advent songs; Christmas candle(s) or Advent wreath

Call to Prayer

LEADER   Emmanuel, you didn't wait until the perfect time to enter our world.

ALL   You came to us when we were most needy.

LEADER   Emmanuel, you didn't come as a powerful ruler.

ALL   You came to us as a child so that we could become children of God.

LEADER   Emmanuel, you didn't come as God, but as a human baby.

ALL   You came to us as a human so we could become divine.

LEADER   Help us know that we can't wait for the perfect time to live our union with you, but help us start right now knowing that we are your children, that you live inside us, that our power is in our union with you.

ALL   With you we can make our world ready for your coming again in glory. Help us take the time to do this, fill our hearts with peace and courage, and make us one with you.

Reading (Matthew 11:2–11)

READER 1   When John heard in prison what the Messiah was doing, he sent word by his disciples and said to him, "Are you the one who is to come, or are we to wait for another?"

READER 2   Jesus answered them, "Go and tell John what you hear and see: the blind receive their sight, the lame walk, the lepers are cleansed, the deaf hear, the dead are raised, and the poor have good news brought to them. And blessed is anyone who takes no offense at me."

READER 3 As they went away, Jesus began to speak to the crowds about John: "What did you go out into the wilderness to look at? A reed shaken by the wind? What then did you go out to see? Someone dressed in soft robes? Look, those who wear soft robes are in royal palaces. What then did you go out to see? A prophet? Yes, I tell you, and more than a prophet. This is the one about whom it is written, 'See, I am sending my messenger ahead of you, who will prepare your way before you.' Truly I tell you, among those born of women no one has arisen greater than John the Baptist; yet the least in the kingdom of heaven is greater than he."

Reflection

LEADER God's reign of peace, justice, and goodness began with the birth of a baby boy. How simple and adorable! No upheaval, no force—just God becoming a child so we could become children of God. Yet how revolutionary! What power! Could there be anything more powerful than God uniting himself with us? Our union with God is so strong that we can make paths straight, fill in valleys, and bring mountains down.

The purpose of the incarnation (God-becoming-human) is our humanity becoming like God. How can we be more like God in the remaining days before Christmas as we take tests, play basketball, practice for concerts, bake cookies, buy and wrap presents, and attend family gatherings?

Who are prophets in our society? How are children and poor persons prophets, even when they have no power? When can you be a prophet? How can you prepare the way of the Lord?

Activities (choose one)

1. Look at a burning Christmas candle or the burning candles of an Advent wreath. Imagine that God is like the flame and you are the candle. As God's warmth and brightness fill you, you become transformed by the flame, consumed by the flame. The flame and candle are one. Meditate for several minutes on Emmanuel, God-with-us. Pray about your vocation to live this union with God. And thank God for this union, God's best Christmas gift to us.

2. Search the words of Advent songs and Christmas carols to find lines about God's union with us. Examples: "He is Emmanuel, the Promised of ages" ("The King of Glory"); "Cast out our sin and enter in, be born in us today" ("O Little Town of Bethlehem"); "Be near me, Lord Jesus; I ask you to stay close by me forever and love me, I pray" ("Away in a Manger"). Incorporate these songs into a prayer service, or make a game of missing words that could be shared with younger students.

Closing Prayer

LEADER   Emmanuel, you came to be one with us. During these busy days before Christmas, teach us amid our frantic rushing to use time to ponder the wonder of your presence among us.

ALL   Help us be grateful for the gifts you have given us, especially your Christmas gift of union with you. When our busyness becomes too great, remind us that our Advent journey will one day lead us to eternal union with you, when there is no time—only love. Amen.

'Tis the Season to Do Good

Theme

Advent reminds us that we live between the "already" and the "not yet," a time when we need to work toward the fullness of God's reign by doing good in imitation of Jesus.

Materials Needed

Art supplies, old Christmas cards with manger scenes, Bibles

Call to Prayer

SIDE 1 "The Lord has made known his victory; he has revealed his vindication in the sight of the nations.

SIDE 2 "He has remembered his steadfast love and faithfulness to the house of Israel.

ALL "All the ends of the earth have seen the victory of our God" (Ps 98).

SIDE 1 "For a child has been born for us, a son given to us; authority rests on his shoulders;

SIDE 2 "and he is named Wonderful Counselor, Mighty God, Everlasting Father, Prince of Peace" (Is 9:6).

ALL O God, as we look at Christmas trees and nativity scenes, remind us that we must continue your steadfast love and faithfulness, your justice and peace.

SIDE 1 Help us do good and bring about right relationships in our world among family members, classmates, the rich and the poor, and all races and cultures. We now live in a season devoted to doing good.

SIDE 2 Please give us courage and conviction so that Christmas is not just one big party or vacation, but a time to bring the fullness of your victory to our broken, darkened world.

ALL Christ be born in us.

Reading (Matthew 1:18–24)

READER 1 Now the birth of Jesus the Messiah took place in this way. When his mother Mary had been engaged to Joseph, but before they lived together, she was found to be with child from the Holy Spirit.

READER 2 Her husband Joseph, being a righteous man and unwilling to expose her to public disgrace, planned to dismiss her quietly. But just when he had resolved to do this, an angel of the Lord appeared to him in a dream and said, "Joseph, son of David, do not be afraid to take Mary as your wife, for the child conceived in her is from the Holy Spirit. She will bear a son, and you are to name him Jesus, for he will save his people from their sins."

READER 3 All this took place to fulfill what had been spoken by the Lord through the prophet: "Look, the virgin shall conceive and bear a son, and they shall name him Emmanuel," which means, "God is with us."

READER 4 When Joseph awoke from sleep, he did as the angel of the Lord commanded him; he took her as his wife, but had no marital relations with her until she had borne a son; and he named him Jesus.

Reflection

LEADER Joseph knew he had to put right what was wrong, but he looked for the very best way—in this case, a quiet way to prevent embarrassment. In this, Joseph is the quintessence of those who know how to live the Advent-Christmas season. Waiting for the Lord, they pray for his coming, but at the same time they are intent on making right what is wrong in the best way possible. This is what the Advent-Christmas season is all about: making right what is wrong and doing it in the best way possible; that is, the way shown by Jesus.

People lived in darkness and sin, longing for the light and goodness of God. In the "right" time God came into the world to help humans be what they are meant to be: reflections of God's glory. Although accomplished fully in Christ, God's plan has not come to fullness. We still await between the "already" achieved in Christ's incarnation and the "not yet" to be achieved in his Second Coming. Since we live between the "already" and the "not yet," it is our responsibility to work toward the fullness of God's reign when all will be right. 'Tis the season to do good.

When someone does something embarrassing, what is the right way to respond? When persons are caught in a sinful action, what is the right way to respond? When persons are involved in wrongdoing such as drinking, smoking, stealing, or gossiping, what is the right way to respond? When persons are burdened with the pressures of Christmas, what is the right way to respond?

Activities (choose one)

1. Prepare several short skits showing how one can do the right thing in activities pertaining to late December, such as gift-giving, parties, attending the last classes before vacation, cleaning the house, spending vacation time with friends, and so on.

2. The birth of Christ means little to us if Christ is not continuing his birth in us. Pretending you are characters in the scenes, slowly read the Infancy Narratives found in Luke and Matthew. Draw yourself in the manger scene and reflect on how Christ would want to be born into your life. (Possibly draw yourself on an old Christmas card that has a manger scene.) Invite your family to draw a manger scene in which they are around the crib. Discuss how Christ continues his incarnation in your family.

Closing Prayer

LEADER   "God of joy, help us sing for joy, for great in our midst is the Holy One of Israel!" (Isaiah 12:6)

SIDE 1   We rejoice, O God, for you give us salvation.

SIDE 2   We rejoice, O God, for you give us health.

SIDE 1   We rejoice, O God, for you gave us your son Jesus.

SIDE 2   We rejoice, O God, for you let us continue your incarnation by setting right what is sinful in our world.

ALL   Please bless our families and friends this Christmas with the fullness you promised. Fill them with peace, strength, and goodness. Let them share in the fullness of your love, "grace upon grace" (John 1:16). Amen.

Icons of God

Theme

Jesus is the image of God, and we are the image of Christ. Just as Christ gave up much to become incarnate, so we must give up much to incarnate Christ in our world today.

Materials Needed

Mirrors, paints, brushes

Call to Prayer

LEADER   Lord Jesus Christ, as we look at manger scenes, we can easily mistake simplicity for weakness. Yet we cannot forget it is you, God Almighty, who once came as a baby in Bethlehem.

ALL   Child of Bethlehem,
Help us become children—the
Requirement of your kingdom.
It amazes us that we share in the very being of God!
Savior and Sacrament of God,
Teach us that we are sacraments—icons—of you,
Measuring our worth by your own gift of self to us.
Awesome God become human, giving God become Bread,
Saving God, make us like you.

Reading (John 1:1–18)

READER 1   In the beginning was the Word, and the Word was with God, and the Word was God. He was in the beginning with God. All things came into being through him, and without him not one thing came into being.

READER 2   What has come into being in him was life, and the life was the light of all people. The light shines in the darkness, and the darkness did not overcome it.

READER 3   There was a man sent from God, whose name was John. He came as a witness to testify to the light, so that all might believe through him. He himself was not the light, but he came to testify to the light. The true light, which enlightens everyone, was coming into the world.

READER 4   He was in the world, and the world came into being through him; yet the world did not know him. He came to what was his own, and his own people did not accept him. But to all who received him, who believed in his name, he gave power to become children of God, who were born, not of blood or of the will of the flesh or of the will of man, but of God.

ALL   And the Word became flesh and lived among us, and we have seen his glory, the glory as of a father's only son, full of grace and truth.

READER 1   John testified to him and cried out, "This was he of whom I said, 'He who comes after me ranks ahead of me because he was before me.'"

READER 2   From his fullness we have all received, grace upon grace.

READER 3   The law indeed was given through Moses; grace and truth came through Jesus Christ.

READER 4   No one has ever seen God. It is God the only Son who is close to the Father's heart, who has made him known.

Reflection

LEADER   As we open Christmas presents, we might wonder what the gifts are worth. Expensive gifts and simple gifts made with love may suggest that we are worth much. We are flattered and humbled by the extravagance of love, time, or money. In a similar way, the prologue of John's gospel tells us that we are worth very much. We are worth God's becoming human, being born in a stable, living the poor life of an itinerant preacher, and hanging several agonizing hours on the cross. We are worth Jesus' whole life in which he gave up the complete intimacy of Trinitarian community for transitory, mortal flesh, becoming human like us in everything except sin.

We are called to be images or icons of Christ. We must do more than imitate, though; we are to incarnate Christ in our lives. This means that just as the Second Person of the Trinity was willing to live among us so we could see and touch him, we must be willing to become like Christ. Others should be able to see and touch Christ in us. This means that we must give up things, as Christ gave up the full intensity of his divinity. We must give up all that will not allow others to see and experience Christ in us; namely, our sins and faults, as well as our negative tendencies.

Christmas may be an occasion to receive gifts that may appeal more to status and ego than meet our needs. Yet Christ became poor so that we could become rich out of his poverty. Trying to be an icon or image of Christ, how can I practice being poor this Christmas season?

The Christmas season contains some of the longest nights of the year. How can I remove "darkness" from people's lives by incarnating the love of Christ?

The incarnation means that Jesus became not only a sacrament of God but also the sacrament of what it means to be human. Jesus continued to grow into full manhood. How am I maturing? Am I developing my full human potential?

Activities (choose one)

1. If you have the courage, take some time during Christmas vacation to sit down (maybe near a Christmas tree) to talk about how you can become more fully human. Ask someone how you can develop your potential.

2. Paint a picture of Jesus on a mirror. Hang it in your bedroom or classroom. When you look in it, remember you are an icon of Christ.

3. Christ taught us to be poor. Give a gift to the needy, possibly a new item of clothing that isn't the right size. Or tithe one-tenth of the money you received as Christmas gifts. Consider giving a donation to a needy organization in the name of a person to whom you'd normally give a gift.

4. Christ came to give hope. Bring hope to someone by contributing to Amnesty International, writing a letter to a prisoner, visiting a sick person, or helping someone in distress (running errands, free babysitting, cleaning, etc.).

Closing Prayer

LEADER   Word made flesh, you brought us tidings of great joy.

ALL   Help us to be tidings of joy and comfort to those who are sick or sad during Christmas.

LEADER   Son of God and Son of Mary, you gave up your glory to make the glory of God known.

ALL   Give us self-sacrificing love and abundant generosity to give up our self-centeredness and egotism.

LEADER   Messiah-Lord, you came in the fullness of time.

ALL   Reveal to us how we can best spend our time during Christmas.

LEADER   Savior-God, give me a star to guide me to you.

ALL   Help us become stars to guide others to you. Amen.

Following Christ Is Risky Business

Theme

Just as the wise men risked much to find the Christ, we take risks to be Christ's followers.

Materials Needed

3 gift boxes, paper, markers

Call to Prayer

LEADER   "Arise, shine; for your light has come, and the glory of the Lord has risen upon you…Nations shall come to your light, and kings to the brightness of your dawn" (Is 60:1, 3).

ALL   O God, we come before you to receive your light and glory.

LEADER   "The grace of God has appeared bringing salvation to all" (Titus 2:11).

ALL   O God, we come to you for grace and salvation.

LEADER   "May he have dominion from sea to sea…. May all kings fall down before him, all nations give him service" (Ps 72:8, 11).

ALL   O God, we bow before you, we give you homage, and we pledge you our service.

Reading (Matthew 2:1–12)

READER 1   In the time of King Herod, after Jesus was born in Bethlehem of Judea, wise men from the East came to Jerusalem, asking, "Where is the child who has been born king of the Jews? For we observed his star at its rising, and we have come to pay him homage."

READER 2   When King Herod heard this, he was frightened, and all Jerusalem with him; and calling together all the chief priests and scribes of the people, he inquired of them where the Messiah was to be born.

READER 3   They told him, "In Bethlehem of Judea; for so it has been written by the prophet: 'And you, Bethlehem, in the land of Judah, are by no means least among the rulers of Judah; for from you shall come a ruler who is to shepherd my people Israel.'"

READER 4   Then Herod secretly called for the wise men and learned from them the exact time when the star had appeared. Then he sent them to Bethlehem, saying, "Go and search diligently for the child; and when you have found him, bring me word so that I may also go and pay him homage."

READER 1   When they had heard the king, they set out; and there, ahead of them, went the star that they had seen at its rising, until it stopped over the place where the child was.

READER 2   When they saw that the star had stopped, they were overwhelmed with joy. On entering the house, they saw the child with Mary his mother; and they knelt down and paid him homage. Then, opening their treasure chests, they offered him gifts of gold, frankincense, and myrrh.

READER 3   And having been warned in a dream not to return to Herod, they left for their own country by another road.

Reflection

LEADER   Ever since the wise men first risked finding the Messiah, people through the ages have risked trying to find Christ. But the risk increases after Christ is found. Doing his Word is a risky adventure. What risks lie in loving one's enemies, picking up crosses, turning the other cheek, laying down lives for one's friends! What would you be willing to risk to know Christ and follow him better? How many miles would you cross to find Christ? What gifts would you bring him?

Activities (choose one)

1. Place three open gift boxes in front of an altar, or make them part of a sacred arrangement for prayer. On three different papers write " I give you the gold of my...," "I give you the frankincense of my...," and "I give you the myrrh of my...." After completing the sentences place your gifts in the three boxes.

2. Spend some time reflecting on yourself as a treasure through which the light of God shines. The light of God plays no favorites, but shines through us no matter who we are. Spend the week treating other persons like treasures.

3. As the Christmas season dissolves into Ordinary Time, offer to help your parish put away Christmas decorations and music. See if any organizations who helped give to the needy in your town during Christmastime need any help.

Closing Prayer

LEADER Lord, you are the Light of the World. Help us carry your light to our darkened world.

ALL At times we don't feel like carrying the light. It's too hard. It's risky business. We'd rather stay uninvolved. Help us, Lord, to be your disciples—persons willing to follow you to the ends of the earth. Amen.

Jesus Is the Norm

Theme

Jesus is the model of all encounters with God. His response to the Father shows how we should respond to God. The way the Father interacts with Jesus in his humanity reveals how God wants to interact with us.

Materials Needed

Baptismal candles, stationery, copy of baptismal vows

Call to Prayer

LEADER God's great love shared with us in baptism has made us part of the great plan of salvation. As we pray, may the Lord open our eyes to see Jesus as the norm of all we do. May we become servants of the Father like Jesus.

ALL We pray for the church that we may be like Jesus, the Servant of God, eager to do the Father's work.

We pray for the world in which we live: may it be a place of respect and concern for the rights of all.

We pray for families torn by hatred and discord: may their homes be healed.

We pray for ourselves that we may live the grace of our baptism by witnessing Christ in word and action.

We pray for all those who have no one to pray for them: give them the blessings they need, and bring persons into their lives who can help them.

Reading (Matthew 3:13–17)

READER 1 Then Jesus came from Galilee to John at the Jordan, to be baptized by him. John would have prevented him, saying, "I need to be baptized by you, and do you come to me?"

READER 2 But Jesus answered him, "Let it be so now; for it is proper for us in this way to fulfill all righteousness." Then he consented.

READER 3 And when Jesus had been baptized, just as he came up from the water, suddenly the heavens were opened to him and he saw the Spirit of God descending like a dove and alighting on him. And a voice from heaven said, "This is my Son, the Beloved, with whom I am well pleased."

Reflection

LEADER Jesus is the full expression of the most profound interaction between God and humanity. What God intended for all his creatures is done in Christ. Jesus becomes, then, the norm for all encounters with God. As we reflect on the interaction between the Father and the Son at Jesus' baptism, we realize a little more how God wants to interact with us and how we can best respond to God.

The voice from heaven speaking of God's pleasure in the Son is a very loving statement similar to Isaiah 42:1 referring to the Servant of Yahweh: "Here is my servant, whom I uphold, my chosen, in whom my soul delights; I have put my spirit upon him." Jesus' mission is defined as serving his Father and doing his will. This servitude, however, is far from slavery; it is an eagerness to please the Father whom the Son loves. Modeling our lives on that of Jesus, we know that we must be servants of God. Do we realize how much God loves us, and does this love make us eager to serve God? Share a time when you were eager to serve God.

The fact that the Spirit alighted or rested on Jesus shows a continuous endowment of Jesus with authority and power from God his Father. We, too, are continuously endowed with power and authority through the grace of baptism and confirmation. God freely shares divine power with us to achieve his plan for the world. Do I use my God-given authority and power to correct wrongdoing, to heal the sick and suffering, to minister in liturgy or elsewhere? Share an experience when you let God's power work in you.

Our close relationship with Christ is expressed in Romans 6, which reminds us we die with Christ and live in Christ because of our baptism. Our own dyings and risings are a participation in Christ's death and resurrection. Our baptism copies the death-resurrection of Jesus. How do you live your baptism? Do you try to die to selfishness and live in the likeness of Christ? Share an experience of dying to your selfishness to be more like Christ.

Activities (choose one)

1. Make a New Year's resolution to be selfless like Christ. Add one act of service to every week in the new year.

2. Renew your baptismal vows. If possible, light your baptismal candle.

3. Write a note of support to the catechumens who will be baptized at the Easter Vigil. Tell them how you try to live your own baptism.

Closing Prayer

LEADER The response is "Keep us faithful to you, Lord Jesus."
When we fail to remember we are anointed by God with power and strength and turn to wrongdoing, (Response.)

When we forget that the Father calls us beloved, (Response.)

When we forget that the norm of our actions and attitudes is the life of Jesus Christ, (Response.)

When we omit prayer for those who will be baptized and for those who have denied their baptismal vows, (Response.)

When we fail to listen to the voice of the Father, (Response.)

When we fail to be open to the Spirit resting upon us, (Response.)

When we think we have done enough praying and good deeds, (Response.)

When we know how much we are loved by the Father, (Response.)

When we know the Father is well pleased with us, (Response.)

ALL   Amen.

Impelled by the Spirit

Theme

Jesus courageously left his hometown to follow the Spirit's lead to a life of ministry. Our own decisions should be directed by the Holy Spirit.

Call to Prayer

LEADER   Holy Spirit of God, as you directed Jesus to begin his public life, give direction to our lives, and give us the courage to carry out what you tell us.

ALL   Give us your wisdom in all decision making. Give us your courage to stand up for our beliefs and live our principles.

LEADER   Strengthen our moral sense to do right despite difficulty.

ALL   Teach us to pray, inspiring us with words and longings. Be our ever-present guide so that we may serve God well.

Reading (John 1:29–34)

READER 1   The next day John saw Jesus coming toward him and declared, "Here is the Lamb of God who takes away the sin of the world! This is he of whom I said, 'After me comes a man who ranks ahead of me because he was before me.' I myself did not know him; but I came baptizing with water for this reason, that he might be revealed to Israel."

READER 2   And John testified, "I saw the Spirit descending from heaven like a dove, and it remained on him. I myself did not know him, but the one who sent me to baptize with water said to me, 'He on whom you see the Spirit descend and remain is the one who baptizes with the Holy Spirit.' And I myself have seen and have testified that this is the Son of God."

Reflection

LEADER   Jesus could have stayed in the carpenter shop, but he made a choice. He knew that people needed the good news more than tables or even all the spiritual good he could have done in his neighborhood. He had to go beyond Nazareth, become an itinerant preacher, and eventually suffer and die. Maybe he saw the hopelessness of the villagers in his hometown and decided it was easier to bear their sins than their despair. Maybe he realized that the people did not know God as a Father and decided it was easier to be condemned for making himself equal to the Father than not revealing the Father at all. Maybe he saw a kingdom and traded his shop to tell people, "The kingdom of God is upon you."

Whatever happened, Jesus chose to leave because he felt compelled to do the will of his Father. He knew that the first thing he had to do was make it known that the Spirit was directing him, as attested by John. After that he would choose his disciples, preach, and work miracles. But for now it was a big enough step just to make it known that he was of God. It was as if he let himself be branded "Religious Person."

What happens when we're branded as "religious"? How does it make you feel? What are occasions when teens need to step out and declare their principles?

Are there any decisions we make that are completely irrevocable or nearly so? How does one make these kinds of decisions? What are steps in serious decision making? How would one go about deciding upon changing one's life, the way Jesus changed from being a carpenter to being a preacher? How will you know what to do after you no longer are a student?

Jesus was impelled by the Holy Spirit to accomplish his role as Messiah. How would you know if you were impelled by the Holy Spirit? How would you know the desires were from God and not from your inner self or the evil spirit?

Activities (choose one)

1. In the month of January we often reflect on ecumenism. Ask religious persons of other faiths how they knew God was leading them. If they are a leader in their church, ask them how they became involved in such leadership. Did they feel driven by the Spirit?

2. In the month of January we often reflect on life issues, such as abortion, euthanasia, and capital punishment. Ask persons of conviction to share their convictions about respect for life. Has their respect for life ever branded them as "religious"?

3. Write an imaginary conversation between two women of Jesus' village who are discussing Jesus recently leaving his hometown.

4. Write a poem titled "Spirit-Driven."

Closing Prayer

LEADER   O Holy Spirit, distinct but inseparable from Father and Son,

ALL   anoint us as you anointed Jesus at the beginning of his public life.

LEADER   Spirit of adoption,

ALL   unite us to God our Father and make us live in God as God's children, crying out Abba, Father!

LEADER Divine Paraclete,

ALL console us and be with us when life is hard.

LEADER Spirit of the Lord,

ALL help us believe Jesus is Lord!

LEADER Fire of God,

ALL transform us by your energy, and descend upon us in a new Pentecost.

LEADER Spirit of God,

ALL impel us by your gifts to use our gifts to build up the kingdom. Amen.

The Good News Isn't Easy

Theme

Many persons in Scripture took risks at God's request. Will we take risks to live the gospel unconditionally?

Materials Needed

Maps or globes

Call to Prayer

LEADER Let us pause to hear God call us by name. (Pause) God, our God, we hear you call us by name, "Come, follow me."

ALL We respond, "Here I am." Whatever you ask, we will do. Help us hear your call each and every day, O God, that we may respond willingly, even eagerly, without counting the cost.

Reading (Matthew 4:12–23)

READER 1 Now when Jesus heard that John had been arrested, he withdrew to Galilee. He left Nazareth and made his home in Capernaum by the sea, in the territory of Zebulun and Naphtali, so that what had been spoken through the prophet Isaiah might be fulfilled:

READER 2 "Land of Zebulun, land of Naphtali, on the road by the sea, across the Jordan, Galilee of the Gentiles—the people who sat in darkness have seen a great light, and for those who sat in the region and shadow of death light has dawned."

READER 3 From that time Jesus began to proclaim, "Repent, for the kingdom of heaven has come near."

READER 4 As he walked by the Sea of Galilee, he saw two brothers, Simon, who is called Peter, and Andrew, his brother, casting a net into the sea—for they were fishermen. And he said to them, "Follow me, and I will make you fish for people."

READER 5 Immediately they left their nets and followed him. As he went from there, he saw two other brothers, James son of Zebedee and his brother John, in the boat with their father Zebedee, mending their nets, and he called them. Immediately they left the boat and their father, and followed him.

Reflection

LEADER   Did you ever notice how often people in Scripture receive a call and within minutes they're on their feet and moving? Mary rose in haste to visit her cousin Elizabeth after God called her through the angel Gabriel. Joseph arose quickly from his dream to flee with Mary and the baby Jesus into Egypt. No matter how many times God called Samuel during the night, he got out of bed to respond. Peter was delivered from prison with the words "Get up quickly." John and James abandoned their family and livelihood without looking back. It seems as if no one thought things through or weighed the consequences or even wondered whether the voices were from God or a messenger of God. Nobody even said, "I must be dreaming"! We might say they were foolish not to calculate the risks or the costs.

Jesus began his ministry by demanding just such foolishness: "Repent!" Turn your lives around! Turn your values upside down! See things from a totally different perspective. Become a child. Become the Body of Christ and let yourself be "eaten." Be light for the world and get burned up in the process. Pick up your cross every day. Change your comfortable life-style. Become a servant. Empty yourself of yourself. Wash feet. Die.

Jesus came to bring good news. But the good news wasn't easy; it was more like disturbing news, unpleasant news, news that would prick consciences. "Repent!" If we had the courage to change, to turn our lives around, to turn our values upside down and live the gospel as it was preached and lived by Jesus Christ—to live the gospel without cutting corners—we would start a revolution.

Discuss the situations given below using the following questions: 1) If you respond to the situation instead of just ignoring it, would you have to change? 2) Would any values need to be turned upside down? 3) Would your response involve any discomfort or suffering, risk or cost?

(a) You hear of a tornado or flood in a nearby city or state.

(b) Your state or country is considering issues that are disrespectful of certain minorities (the unborn, immigrants, prisoners, illegal aliens, the aged, certain ethnic groups, the terminally ill).

(c) Your best friend accidentally kills someone and is accused of vehicular homicide.

(e) Most of your classmates cheat by copying homework, and you have an opportunity to copy, too.

(f) You have turned away from God in a serious way such as abortion, repeated absence from Sunday worship, premarital sex, drinking, or gambling.

(g) You are asked to give up spring break to help the needy in Appalachia or in an inner city.

(h) Your school has a tutoring program and requests your help as a tutor three nights a week.

(i) You feel in your heart that God wants you to read Scripture and/or pray more every day.

(j) You sense that you are becoming addicted to the computer.

Activities (choose one)

1. Role play some of the situations listed above by having a conversation with God. Example: "God, you really want me to pray more every day?"

2. On a globe or map write values that need to be turned upside down so that our world can be a better place in the new millennium. On a second globe or map write values that you hope will prevail in the new millennium.

3. As a class, decide to do something that involves a risk, such as praying over a sick person, giving a program or providing a dance in a nursing home, or making a request to the principal.

Closing Prayer

LEADER   Please respond: "Here I am, Lord. Send me."
When you need someone to comfort the sick…(Response.)

When you need someone to give food, clothes, or money…(Response.)

When you need someone to help a student with math…(Response.)

When you need a young person to be involved in church activities… (Response.)

When you need someone to give a smile…(Response.)

When you need someone to challenge wrongdoing…(Response.)

When you need someone to stop a friend from drinking too much… (Response.)

When you need someone to visit the homebound…(Response.)

When you need someone to be a leader to change the world's economic and social ills…(Response.)

And when you just need someone to stop in chapel or church to say hello to you in your eucharistic presence…(Response.)

ALL   Amen.

Being on God's Team

Theme

The beatitudes are a moral revolution. If the disciples of Christ live them as a team, Christians could change society.

Materials Needed

Bibles, individual beatitudes written on papers and put in a box

Call to Prayer

LEADER   Coach Jesus, we are your team. Sometimes we play well and hard, and we give you praise for giving us the grace to lead good lives.

ALL   We thank you for giving us the courage to follow you, even when we may suffer for it. We glorify you for the times our friends and families united as a team to show we were your followers.

LEADER   But sometimes we forget the team rules, we don't live your gospel slogans, and we show poor team spirit.

ALL   Please forgive us, and we ask your gift of wisdom now as we pray and study your game plan, the beatitudes.

Reading (Matthew 5:1–12)

READER 1   When Jesus saw the crowds, he went up the mountain; and after he sat down, his disciples came to him. Then he began to speak, and taught them, saying:

READER 2   "Blessed are the poor in spirit, for theirs is the kingdom of heaven.

READER 3   "Blessed are those who mourn, for they will be comforted.

READER 2   "Blessed are the meek, for they will inherit the earth.

READER 3   "Blessed are those who hunger and thirst for righteousness, for they will be filled.

READER 2   "Blessed are the merciful, for they will receive mercy.

READER 3   "Blessed are the pure in heart, for they will see God.

READER 2 "Blessed are the peacemakers, for they will be called children of God.

READER 3 "Blessed are those who are persecuted for righteousness' sake, for theirs is the kingdom of heaven.

READER 2 "Blessed are you when people revile you and persecute you and utter all kinds of evil against you falsely on my account.

READER 1 "Rejoice and be glad, for your reward is great in heaven, for in the same way they persecuted the prophets who were before you."

Reflection

LEADER Your team coaches and your organizations' moderators probably give you a slogan or a few statements that spell out for you exactly what they expect of you as a member of that team or organization. Or you may have constitutions or a point system delineating exactly what is expected of you to be in good standing. In a way Jesus gives the beatitudes to us, his disciples, as that kind of guideline. It is as if Jesus says, "These are the essential characteristics of a disciple of mine. If you're on my team, do these things."

The beatitudes sound so simple: be a peacemaker, be merciful, work for justice. Yet they spell out a moral revolution that rocked the world in Jesus' time and still rock the world today wherever they are lived in their fullness. These principles opposed many of the conventional values of the Jewish and Roman world of Jesus' day, and they still are in direct opposition to the values of many governments, most advertisements, and many persons today.

Living these beatitudes makes us anomalies, persons who live so differently from the normal way that we stand out. Of course, standing out is something we usually don't like to do; but let's face it, in many ways we live in an unchristian world, and when the world sees any of us being real Christians, it notices. What advertisement, for example, promises happiness by being poor in spirit (not showing off our wealth, giving deference to others, being content with what we have)? What government calls its citizens to put their complete trust in God rather than weapons and the stock market? What professional athletic team promotes forgiveness and compassion?

The beatitudes come early in the gospel. It is as if they herald the rest of the good news and call forth the beginning of the reign of God. In what ways are the beatitudes good news?

If the beatitudes are the charter or constitution of the reign of God, then we must live them daily. What are some ways we can live the beatitudes in school and at home?

On a scale of 1–10, how well is our society practicing these beatitudes? For God's kingdom to come, what changes would you suggest in our society to bring about the fullness of the reign of God? What could we do to become better players on God's team?

Activities (choose one)

1. Write a pep talk or motivational speech that Jesus might give to his team of disciples. Use as many phrases from the beatitudes as you can.

2. The general statements of the beatitudes are further explained by many concrete examples from the life of Jesus. Divide into groups, each group taking two beatitudes. Search the four gospels to find concrete examples of mercy, meekness, efforts to achieve justice, persecution, etc. (Alternative: Divide the blackboard into nine parts for the nine times the word "Blessed" is used in Matthew 5:1–12. Under each statement list Scripture passages that correspond, or write practical ways the beatitude can be lived today.)

3. Divide into groups of about 5–6 students. Select a beatitude from a box. Prepare a skit to show how that beatitude could be practiced today. (Alternative: Write a 30-second commercial for radio or television promoting the beatitude.)

Closing Prayer

LEADER Coach Jesus, we have just reflected on your game plan and rule book. We know what we have to do.

ALL Help us each day to practice the beatitudes so that we can preach the gospel with our lives. May all people know we are your followers by our mercy, trust, purity of heart, peacemaking, and perseverance under persecution. Amen.

Salt and Light

Theme

What Christ was we must be. Like Christ, we must be salt and light, flavoring and illuminating everyday situations.

Materials Needed

Drawing paper, Bibles, blessed salt, candle stubs or tapers

Call to Prayer

LEADER Lord Jesus Christ, you are the Light of the World. Help us to know you, that we may not walk in darkness.

ALL Transform us into your light that we too may be lights for the world.

LEADER Show us your glory that we may shine with your presence.

ALL Help us now that we may reflect on you as light and salt, so that we may become light and salt for others.

Reading (Matthew 5:13–16)

READER 1 Jesus said to his disciples: "You are the salt of the earth; but if salt has lost its taste, how can its saltiness be restored? It is no longer good for anything, but is thrown out and trampled under foot.

READER 2 "You are the light of the world. A city built on a hill cannot be hid. No one after lighting a lamp puts it under the bushel basket, but on the lampstand, and it gives light to all in the house.

READER 3 "In the same way, let your light shine before others, so that they may see your good works and give glory to your Father in heaven."

Reflection

LEADER Our Christian life is a process of conversion into Christ. What Christ was we must be. Christ came as light into a world darkened by sin and as salt into a world whose values had become bland and tasteless.

This passage reminds us that religion is real when it becomes our everyday experience. We can be light and salt at a basketball game, in a shopping mall, on the job, during a party, or in a classroom. But for people to see the light or taste the salt we must become light and salt; in other words, we must allow Christ's light to shine through us, so that Christ's way of acting can flavor our own actions. Our challenge is to become Christ the light and Christ the salt.

How can we become more transparent so that Christ's light can shine through us? How can we let Christ flavor our actions?

Activities (choose one)

1. What follows this gospel passage are practical ways to be salt and light. List practical ways to be salt and light from Matthew, chapters 5–7.

2. Draw yourself as a heart with a candle in the middle. Around the heart list or draw many of the places you frequent each week, such as your classroom, the mall, your place of employment, a fast-food restaurant, etc. Let the rays of the candle's light touch these places. Reflect on practical ways Christ's light can illumine these places through you.

3. Give each student a small amount of blessed salt (about a teaspoonful). As a class, pray that evil will be driven from all places where the students live, work, and go to school. In the course of the week, students unobtrusively sprinkle blessed salt in places that seem to need evil dispelled.

Closing Prayer

If possible, give each student a candle stub or taper (possibly those used at the previous Easter Vigil). Light it from a large candle (possibly the Paschal candle).

ALL   Lord Jesus Christ, you are the Light of the World, and you call us to be light and salt for others. As we go about our week, illuminate any dark places we may enter with your light shining through us. Amen.

Listen to a song about light while watching the candle burn.

Are Minimum Daily Requirements Enough?

Theme

Christ's demands stretch us beyond the moral minimum.

Materials Needed

Art materials needed to make promises of prayer or certificates of service

Call to Prayer

LEADER   The following prayer is based on "A Prayer for Inner Contentment," written by Saint Thomas More in the sixteenth century.

ALL   Lord, give us holy hearts that always see what is the best.

LEADER   When in positions of doubt, fear, or evil, do not let us become frightened. With your help we can overcome our difficulties and bring order where there is confusion.

ALL   Give us hearts that are never bored, because they are turned inward on ourselves. But rather turn our hearts outward, where they can become excited to see what they can do for others. And give us a sense of humor that our hearts may always be happy.

Reading (Matthew 5:17–37)

READER 1   Jesus said to his disciples, "Do not think that I have come to abolish the law or the prophets; I have come not to abolish but to fulfill. For truly I tell you, until heaven and earth pass away, not one letter, not one stroke of a letter, will pass from the law until all is accomplished. Therefore, whoever breaks one of the least of these commandments, and teaches others to do the same, will be called least in the kingdom of heaven; but whoever does them and teaches them will be called great in the kingdom of heaven. For I tell you, unless your righteousness exceeds that of the scribes and Pharisees, you will never enter the kingdom of heaven.

READER 2   "You have heard that it was said to those of ancient times, 'You shall not murder,' and 'whoever murders shall be liable to judgment.' But I say to you that if you are angry with a brother or sister, you will be liable to judgment; and if you insult a brother or sister, you will be liable to the council; and if you say, 'You fool,' you will be liable to the hell of fire.

READER 3 "So when you are offering your gift at the altar, if you remember that your brother or sister has something against you, leave your gift there before the altar and go; first be reconciled to your brother or sister, and then come and offer your gift.

READER 4 "Come to terms quickly with your accuser while you are on the way to court with him, or your accuser may hand you over to the judge, and the judge to the guard, and you will be thrown into prison. Truly I tell you, you will never get out until you have paid the last penny.

READER 5 "You have heard that it was said, 'You shall not commit adultery.' But I say to you that everyone who looks at a woman with lust has already committed adultery with her in his heart.

READER 6 "If your right eye causes you to sin, tear it out and throw it away; it is better for you to lose one of your members than for your whole body to be thrown into hell. And if your right hand causes you to sin, cut it off and throw it away; it is better for you to lose one of your members than for your whole body to go into hell.

READER 7 "It was also said, 'Whoever divorces his wife, let him give her a certificate of divorce.' But I say to you that anyone who divorces his wife, except on the ground of unchastity, causes her to commit adultery; and whoever marries a divorced woman commits adultery.

READER 8 "Again, you have heard that it was said to those of ancient times, 'You shall not swear falsely, but carry out the vows you have made to the Lord.' But I say to you, do not swear at all, either by heaven, for it is the throne of God, or by the earth, for it is his footstool, or by Jerusalem, for it is the city of the great King. And do not swear by your head, for you cannot make one hair white or black. Let your word be 'Yes, yes' or 'No, No'; anything more than this comes from the evil one."

Reflection

LEADER Matthew's audience consisted of Jews who respected and loved Moses. Without diminishing the Law of Moses, Matthew expertly portrays the radical commandments of Christ. Those of Christ require much more risk and much greater love so that God's will may be done perfectly. They require emptying ourselves of our self-centeredness and filling the needs of others. They require letting go of our "rights"—our right to be angry, our right to divorce, our right to take an oath, our right to do the minimum that the law demands. They require excavating our hearts to make room for the love of Christ to fill them. They require letting Christ grow to his full stature in us.

How can we empty ourselves of our self-centeredness?

When do you most want to demand your rights? Does relinquishing one's rights make a person holy or weak?

How can Christ grow to his full stature in us?

What more can we do to live our baptism than follow the commandments?

Activities (choose one)

1. Write cheers based on the meaning in the gospel passage above. Use contrasting statements. Example: "Don't do the minimum! Always do the maximum! All for Christ! Christ for all!" or "Give me an M! Give me an O! Give me an R! Give me an E! What does Christ want? More!"

2. Make Valentines that include certificates of service or promises of prayer. Give these to homebound relatives.

3. Write commercials for spiritual vitamins. The minimum daily moral requirements are insufficient for the strong Christian.

Closing Prayer

LEADER   Heart of Christ, make our hearts like yours.

SIDE 1   Give us big hearts that can expand to your generous outpouring of love.

SIDE 2   Give us sensitive hearts attuned to the needs of others.

SIDE 1   Give us warm hearts that reach out to friends and family in ever more creative ways as we mature.

SIDE 2   Give us enlightened hearts that we may know how to do your will perfectly.

SIDE 1   Give us faithful hearts that never tire doing good.

SIDE 2   Give us sincere hearts to speak the truth.

ALL   Jesus, meek and humble of heart, make our hearts like yours, always eager to do more. Amen.

Lent's Purpose: Union with God

Theme

The temptations of Jesus show that Jesus wanted one thing: union with God. Lent is a season that can help us attain union with God.

Materials Needed

Paper and markers, list of activities regarding the Elect, Bibles

Call to Prayer

LEADER   Please respond: "All we need is you, Jesus."
When we are tempted to think we need more honors, let us remember… (Response.)

When we are tempted to think we need the approval of others, let us remember… (Response.)

When we are tempted to think we have to have everything under control, let us remember… (Response.)

When we think life would be so much better if we had more money or power or success, let us remember… (Response.)

When we trust in stockpiles of weapons, let us remember… (Response.)

When everything is going well in our life and we think we don't need God or anyone else, let us remember… (Response.)

When we begin Lent and think we have to add many difficult things to do, let us remember… (Response.)

Reading (Matthew 4:1–11)

READER 1   Then Jesus was led up by the Spirit into the wilderness to be tempted by the devil. He fasted forty days and forty nights, and afterwards he was famished.

READER 2   The tempter came and said to him, "If you are the Son of God, command these stones to become loaves of bread." But he answered, "It is written, 'One does not live by bread alone, but by every word that comes from the mouth of God.'"

READER 3   Then the devil took him to the holy city and placed him on the pinnacle of the temple, saying to him, "If you are the Son of God, throw yourself down; for it is written, 'He will command his angels concerning you,' and 'On their hands they will bear you up, so that you will not dash your foot against a stone.'"

READER 4 Again, the devil took him to a very high mountain and showed him all the kingdoms of the world and their splendor; and he said to him, "All these I will give you, if you will fall down and worship me." Jesus said to him, "Away with you, Satan! for it is written, 'Worship the Lord your God, and serve only him.'"

READER 5 Then the devil left him, and suddenly angels came and waited on him.

Reflection

LEADER Jesus underwent some of the most severe temptations humans can ever experience: the need for approval, the need to be right, and the need to have everything under control. Aren't these temptations some of our worst ones, too? Jesus resisted by allowing himself to go deeper. What did Jesus really want down deep? It wasn't making a crowd say, "Wow!" It wasn't showing moral superiority. It wasn't aligning himself with the rich and famous. Deep down Jesus wanted only one thing: union with God.

Lent reminds us that our baptism incorporates us into the paschal event of Jesus. What are some things that will require dying to yourself in order to rid yourself of an excessive desire for approval, control, and success?

Lent is a time to take a spiritual stance. It is a time to look deeply within ourselves to see what motivates us. Am I focusing too much attention on any one person or thing? Am I overly concerned about myself, my image, my health, my success? Do I fill my day with important things, or do I surround myself with the trivial? Am I alert to the workings of God, or am I dulled and drugged by things that prevent me from leading a Christian life? Do I really desire union with God?

Lent calls: Pick up your cross and follow Jesus. Will you respond to that call? Will you be willing to get rid of the unimportant and trivial? Will you be willing to be open to a new way to love, a new openness to others, a new eagerness to serve? Will you see fasting, almsgiving, and prayer not so much as spiritual athletics, but as a way to get to the core of your being, to discover more ways to say, "It is no longer I who live, but it is Christ who lives in me" (Gal 2:20)? Will Lent be a time to deepen your union with God?

Sometimes people add a lot of things to Lent: prayer, fasting, almsgiving. However, these things are not "additives"; they are essentials of Christianity. What are some things you could begin in Lent but continue throughout the year?

Activities (choose one)

1. Draw a desert as both a place of demons and a place to meet God. Label it

"Kenosis Desert." (*Kenosis* is a Greek word that suggests emptying ourselves so that we can be filled with God.) Possibly portray a meeting with a devil or with God.

2. Paraphrase Matthew 4:1–11 to show God or an angel suggesting three positive ways to attain union with God. Put yourself in the place of Jesus, and respond to these positive "temptations."

3. Plan to participate in the various events involving the Elect as they prepare for the Easter sacraments; for example, the Rite of Election, scrutinies, a retreat, or practice for the Easter Vigil. Ask the moderator of the RCIA if there is anything your class could do to help, such as serving refreshments, making place favors, or writing letters of encouragement.

Closing Prayer

LEADER Let us pray that we may spend the days of Lent well.

ALL O God of love and mystery, your son Jesus showed us how to live.

LEADER Through his resistance of temptation, give us strength. Through his service to the poor, open our eyes to their needs.

ALL Through his ability to make wise decisions, help us know what you want of us. Through his dying, help us die to our selfishness and sin. Through his rising, help us be the best we can be.

LEADER Through his humanity, help us be fully human. Through his divine nature, deepen our union with you.

ALL We ask this in the grace and power of the Holy Spirit. Amen.

There's Always Room for Dessert

Theme

Mystical experiences are part of the Christian's life.

Materials Needed

Paper, pencils or markers

Call to Prayer

LEADER   God, we seek to find you in all things.

ALL   We place all our trust in you.

LEADER   Help us to become quiet, so that we can hear your voice. Help us become open to whatever you want us to do.

ALL   Make us eager to hear your voice.

LEADER   Let us bask in the sunshine of your radiant face.

ALL   And open our hearts to receive you whenever and wherever you come to us.

LEADER   Lead us up the mountain or walk with us on level ground.

ALL   Wherever you go, we will follow, seeing you above all else.

Reading (Matthew 17:1–9)

READER 1   Six days later, Jesus took with him Peter and James and his brother John and led them up a high mountain, by themselves. And he was transfigured before them, and his face shone like the sun, and his clothes became dazzling white.

READER 2   Suddenly there appeared to them Moses and Elijah, talking with him. Then Peter said to Jesus, "Lord, it is good for us to be here; if you wish, I will make three dwellings here, one for you, one for Moses, and one for Elijah."

READER 3   While he was still speaking, suddenly a bright cloud overshadowed them, and from the cloud a voice said, "This is my Son, the Beloved; with him I am well pleased; listen to him!"

READER 4 When the disciples heard this, they fell to the ground and were overcome by fear. But Jesus came and touched them, saying, "Get up and do not be afraid." And when they looked up, they saw no one except Jesus himself alone.

READER 5 As they were coming down the mountain, Jesus ordered them, "Tell no one about the vision until after the Son of Man has been raised from the dead."

Reflection

LEADER The story of the Transfiguration rests upon a mystical experience of the disciples. In some indescribable way they experienced God's presence in the bright cloud similar to the *shekinah,* God's visible presence to the Hebrews wandering in the desert. This mystical experience filled them with awe and wonder, and they did not want the experience to end.

Occasionally you may have experienced God in such a mystical way. Maybe you were praying, and the time seemed to go very quickly. Or maybe you were singing a hymn, and you felt very moved by the melody and words. Maybe you meditated on Scripture, and you really felt that you were part of the scene. Maybe you were kneeling in a quiet chapel or praying in your bedroom and felt very loved by the Lord. Maybe you experienced great emotional pain, but you "heard" a voice telling you that things would be all right.

Such events are quite normal for the Christian. God is always surrounding us with love, but sometimes we are more attuned, and the love overwhelms us. God is always present, but sometimes we feel God's presence more closely. These mystical experiences are the desserts in our Christian diet or the pleasant meadows on our Christian journey. Such spiritual "highs" are God's way of drawing us closer. Once we experience them, we want more. There's always room for such spiritual "desserts."

The Transfiguration enabled Jesus to walk the way to Jerusalem and the cross. What enables you to be able to face difficult situations? How does your faith help you in suffering?

Have you ever prayed spontaneously with anyone besides your family? Have you ever asked someone, "Could I pray with you?" When you see people in pain, have you ever reached out to them by taking their hand and asking, "May I pray over you?" Praying with someone or praying over someone is a gift we all have in virtue of our baptism, but like all gifts they must be exercised. Do you think the next time you see your friend depressed or your teammate injured that you could pray over them? You could be an instrument of God's healing.

Activities (choose one)

1. Draw a well-balanced meal. Label each dish with some aspect of your Catholic faith. What is the "meat" of your spiritual life? What are the "potatoes"? What are the "side dishes"? What is the "dessert"? What provides "drink"?

2. Spend some time in a very quiet place. Imagine yourself surrounded by God's love, care, and concern.

3. Invite someone to speak on healing.

Closing Prayer

LEADER May Jesus live in us!

ALL Eternal Light, shine into our darkened hearts. Radiant God, help us spread your glow.

LEADER Overwhelm us with your love and concern so that we never doubt your nearness.

ALL When we feel your presence, let us be grateful. When it seems that you are far away, give us faith.

LEADER Say to us as you said of Jesus your Son, "This is my beloved in whom I am well pleased."

ALL Then may we grow into your transfigured glory. Amen.

True Worship = Living the Life of Jesus

Theme

Liturgy is living. True worship is living the life of Jesus.

Call to Prayer

LEADER   We delight in you, Lord, with all our being.

ALL   You deserve our highest praise. To your greatness we surrender.

LEADER   May our prayer rise like incense before you. May our reflection bring us closer to you.

ALL   Make our lives a living liturgy in imitation of you.

LEADER   May our faith, hope, and love be our sacrifice of thanksgiving.

ALL   Holy God, Holy Mighty One, Holy Immortal One, have mercy on us.

Reading (John 4:5–42)

READER 1   Jesus came to a Samaritan city called Sychar, near the plot of ground that Jacob had given to his son Joseph. Jacob's well was there, and Jesus, tired out by his journey, was sitting by the well. It was about noon.

READER 2   A Samaritan woman came to draw water, and Jesus said to her, "Give me a drink." (His disciples had gone to the city to buy food.) The Samaritan woman said to him, "How is it that you, a Jew, ask a drink of me, a woman of Samaria?" (Jews do not share things in common with Samaritans.)

READER 3   Jesus answered her, "If you knew the gift of God, and who it is that is saying to you, 'Give me a drink,' you would have asked him, and he would have given you living water." The woman said to him, "Sir, you have no bucket, and the well is deep. Where do you get that living water? Are you greater than our ancestor Jacob, who gave us the well, and with his sons and his flocks drank from it?"

READER 4   Jesus said to her, "Everyone who drinks of this water will be thirsty again, but those who drink of the water that I will give them will never be thirsty. The water that I will give will become in them a spring of water gushing up to eternal life." The woman said to him, "Sir, give me this water, so that I may never be thirsty or have to keep coming here to draw water."

READER 1   Jesus said to her, "Go, call your husband, and come back." The woman answered him, "I have no husband." Jesus said to her, "You are right in saying, 'I have no husband'; for you have had five husbands, and the one you have now is not your husband. What you have said is true!" The woman said to him, "Sir, I see that you are a prophet. Our ancestors worshiped on this mountain, but you say that the place where people must worship is in Jerusalem."

READER 2   Jesus said to her, "Woman, believe me, the hour is coming when you will worship the Father neither on this mountain nor in Jerusalem. You worship what you do not know; we worship what we know, for salvation is from the Jews. But the hour is coming, and is now here, when the true worshipers will worship the Father in spirit and truth, for the Father seeks such as these to worship him. God is spirit, and those who worship him must worship in spirit and truth."

READER 3   The woman said to him, "I know that Messiah is coming" (who is called Christ). "When he comes, he will proclaim all things to us." Jesus said to her, "I am he, the one who is speaking to you."

READER 4   Just then his disciples came. They were astonished that he was speaking with a woman, but no one said, "What do you want?" or, "Why are you speaking with her?" Then the woman left her water jar and went back to the city. She said to the people, "Come and see a man who told me everything I have ever done! He cannot be the Messiah, can he?" They left the city and were on their way to him.

READER 1   Meanwhile the disciples were urging him, "Rabbi, eat something." But he said to them, "I have food to eat that you do not know about." So the disciples said to one another, "Surely no one has brought him something to eat?" Jesus said to them, "My food is to do the will of him who sent me and to complete his work. Do you not say, 'Four months more, then comes the harvest'? But I tell you, look around you, and see how the fields are ripe for harvesting. The reaper is already receiving wages, and is gathering fruit for eternal life, so that sower and reaper may rejoice together. For here the saying holds true, 'One sows and another reaps.' I sent you to reap that for which you did not labor. Others have labored, and you have entered into their labor."

READER 2   Many Samaritans from that city believed in him because of the woman's testimony, "He told me everything I have ever done." So when the Samaritans came to him, they asked him to stay with them; and he stayed there two days. And many more believed because of his word. They said to the woman, "It is no longer because of what you said that we believe, for we have heard for ourselves, and we know that this is truly the Savior of the world."

Reflection

LEADER No rabbi would talk to a woman, even a wife or daughter, in public. But Jesus talked to the Samaritan woman at a time when the quarrel between Jews and Samaritans was still smoldering after four hundred years. Breaking down barriers, Jesus gave us a universal gospel. God so loved the world that he would not allow for divisions. The Messiah came for all. Jesus was always ready to sit down with anyone.

His openness to people added truth to his words about worship. As man, Christ is the supreme worship of the Father. His life was perfect worship. If our life is one of faith, hope, and love, then we can participate in meaningful liturgy. True liturgy is what is going on in people. It is to live the same life as Jesus did. Liturgy ritualizes the pattern of Christ-in-us.

Our true worship of God is to accept the salvation he gives us. Are you open to salvation? Do you follow the inspirations of the Holy Spirit? Can you sense when it is time to receive the Sacrament of Reconciliation?

Liturgy celebrates Christ-in-us. Are you open to all people of every race, class, and religion as Jesus was? Do you exclude classmates or teammates?

Activities (choose one)

1. Prepare and participate in a Sacrament of Reconciliation.

2. Think of someone you dislike and ostracize. Picture yourself as that person. Find in your heart some compassion for him or her. (If this person is a family member, wear his or her shoes for ten minutes to feel what it would be like to fill them.)

Closing Prayer

LEADER We worship you, O Lord.

ALL Humbly we bow before you. We are your servants who come before you as Servant of God. Teach us your humility.

LEADER We worship you, O Lord.

ALL Humbly we bow before you. We are your followers who look to you for guidance. Teach us your wisdom.

LEADER We worship you, O Lord.

ALL Humbly we bow before you. We are those who are redeemed by your blood. We thank you for the victory of your cross. Teach us its meaning. Amen.

Bold Christians

Theme

Christians must be bold in expressing and living their faith.

Materials Needed

Blindfolds, computer

Call to Prayer *(based on Ephesians 5:8–9)*

LEADER   Before we were baptized, we lived in darkness.

ALL   Now we are light in the Lord.

LEADER   "Live as children of light—for the fruit of the light is found in all that is good and right and true."

ALL   May we see how we can best live our faith and do it with boldness, not hesitating under peer pressure or self-consciousness. O God, we place our faith in you. Enlighten us that we may always do what is good, honest, and right.

Reading (John 9:1–41)

READER 1   As Jesus walked along, he saw a man blind from birth. His disciples asked him, "Rabbi, who sinned, this man or his parents, that he was born blind?"

READER 2   Jesus answered, "Neither this man nor his parents sinned; he was born blind so that God's work might be revealed in him. We must work the works of him who sent me while it is day; night is coming when no one can work. As long as I am in the world, I am the light of the world."

READER 3   When he had said this, he spat on the ground and made mud with the saliva and spread the mud on the man's eyes, saying to him, "Go, wash in the pool of Siloam" (which means Sent). Then he went and washed and came back able to see.

READER 4   The neighbors and those who had seen him before as a beggar began to ask, "Is this not the man who used to sit and beg?" Some were saying, "It is he." Others were saying, "No, but it is someone like him." He kept saying, "I am the man." But they kept asking him, "Then how were your eyes opened?" He answered, "The man called Jesus made mud, spread it on my eyes, and said to me, 'Go to Siloam and wash.' Then I went and washed and received my sight." They said to him, "Where is he?" He said, "I do not know."

READER 5 They brought to the Pharisees the man who had formerly been blind. Now it was a sabbath day when Jesus made the mud and opened his eyes. Then the Pharisees also began to ask him how he had received his sight. He said to them, "He put mud on my eyes. Then I washed, and now I see."

READER 6 Some of the Pharisees said, "This man is not from God, for he does not observe the sabbath." But others said, "How can a man who is a sinner perform such signs?" And they were divided. So they said again to the blind man, "What do you say about him? It was your eyes he opened." He said, "He is a prophet."

READER 1 The Jews did not believe that he had been blind and had received his sight until they called the parents of the man who had received his sight and asked them, "Is this your son, who you say was born blind? How then does he now see?" His parents answered, "We know that this is our son, and that he was born blind; but we do not know how it is that now he sees, nor do we know who opened his eyes. Ask him; he is of age. He will speak for himself." His parents said this because they were afraid of the Jews; for the Jews had already agreed that anyone who confessed Jesus to be the Messiah would be put out of the synagogue. Therefore his parents said, "He is of age; ask him."

READER 2 So for the second time they called the man who had been blind, and they said to him, "Give glory to God! We know that this man is a sinner." He answered, "I do not know whether he is a sinner. One thing I do know, that though I was blind, now I see." They said to him, "What did he do to you? How did he open your eyes?" He answered them, "I have told you already, and you would not listen. Why do you want to hear it again? Do you also want to become his disciples?"

READER 3 Then they reviled him, saying, "You are his disciple, but we are disciples of Moses. We know that God has spoken to Moses, but as for this man, we do not know where he comes from." The man answered, "Here is an astonishing thing! You do not know where he comes from, and yet he opened my eyes. We know that God does not listen to sinners, but he does listen to one who worships him and obeys his will. Never since the world began has it been heard that anyone opened the eyes of a person born blind. If this man were not from God, he could do nothing." They answered him, "You were born entirely in sins, and are you trying to teach us?" And they drove him out.

READER 4 Jesus heard that they had driven him out, and when he found him, he said, "Do you believe in the Son of Man?" He answered, "And who is he, sir? Tell me, so that I may believe in him." Jesus said to him, "You have seen him, and the one speaking with you is he." He said, "Lord, I believe." And he worshiped him.

READER 5   Jesus said, "I came into this world for judgment so that those who do not see may see, and those who do see may become blind." Some of the Pharisees near him heard this and said to him, "Surely we are not blind, are we?" Jesus said to them, "If you were blind, you would not have sin. But now that you say, 'We see,' your sin remains."

Reflection

LEADER   Jesus was sent by the Father to give light, and it was at Siloam (a word meaning sent) that sight was restored. But the miracle is only one part of the gospel passage. Much of the story deals with the smugness of the Pharisees and the boldness of the man born blind. As such, it is a story for us who must be bold Christians.

Like the man born blind, do we believe actively? Is our faith something we do and become, or is it just something we've had since we were baptized? Is our faith more than a list of beliefs? Is it a personal relationship with God?

The faith of the man born blind made him bold in declaring several times that Jesus cured him, despite the implicit threat that he would be thrown out of the temple. He even goes so far as to chide the Pharisees, the religious leaders, for their failure to see. "Now who's blind?" he seems to ask. He boldly claims that Jesus has to be from God. Then when Jesus tells him that this is a fact, he worships him.

The blindness of the Pharisees did not allow them to see beyond their surface belief that any malady was God's punishment. They assumed the man born blind was a sinner who would know nothing of God and spiritual things. From where would such a false assumption come? Had they never associated with persons with disabilities? Were they threatened by the disability? In rejecting the man born blind, they were, in effect, rejecting Jesus.

Are there persons whom we reject? What are the root causes leading to rejection? Do we surround ourselves with persons who are like ourselves? Who are outcasts in our area? Can we see these outsiders as "sacraments of the eternally rejected Christ"?* How would we respond if they claimed to have more faith in Jesus than we have?

Are we willing to be bold about our faith? If someone is hurt, do we offer to pray over them or for them? If friends say they are not going to church or praying, do we share our own belief in religious practices? If classmates are cheating, doing drugs, shoplifting, or participating in other sinful actions, are we willing to try to stop such activities?

Activities (choose one)

1. Make a computer-banner about faith for the classroom. It might say, "Have faith. Live faith. Share faith."

2. Step out in faith to share your faith. Challenge each other to share your faith in some way throughout the week. Next week share your stories.

Closing Prayer

LEADER   O God, increase our faith.

SIDE 1   Help us to see that we need to be open to others who are different from us.

SIDE 2   Help us to see that our faith is more than something we have; it is something we do.

SIDE 1   Help us to see that faith is our trust in you.

SIDE 2   Help us to see that we need to become more bold in living our faith.

ALL   Give us courage to have faith, live faith, and share faith. Amen.

Radical Grace: Daily Meditations by Richard Rohr, John Bookser Feister, ed. (Cincinnati, OH: St. Anthony Messenger Press, 1995), p. 354.

W.W.J.D.

Theme

We need to study the life of Christ to determine what Jesus would have done in our present-day situations.

Call to Prayer

LEADER   As we come toward the end of our lenten journey and prepare for the most sacred time of the year, Lord Jesus Christ, we beg you to help us become more and more like you.

ALL   Through the fasting, prayer, and almsgiving of Lent, help us become more like you, Lord Jesus Christ, who taught us to pray. Make our thoughts like your thoughts, and our words and actions like yours.

LEADER   Having become your body in baptism, may we become ever more the Body of Christ through partaking of your sacramental body and blood.

ALL   Keep ever before our minds the question "What would Jesus do?"

Reading (John 11:1–45)

READER 1   Now a certain man was ill, Lazarus of Bethany, the village of Mary and her sister Martha. Mary was the one who anointed the Lord with perfume and wiped his feet with her hair; her brother Lazarus was ill. So the sisters sent a message to Jesus, "Lord, he whom you love is ill." But when Jesus heard it, he said, "This illness does not lead to death; rather it is for God's glory, so that the Son of God may be glorified through it." Accordingly, though Jesus loved Martha and her sister and Lazarus, after having heard that Lazarus was ill, he stayed two days longer in the place where he was.

READER 2   Then after this he said to the disciples, "Let us go to Judea again." The disciples said to him, "Rabbi, the Jews were just now trying to stone you, and are you going there again?" Jesus answered, "Are there not twelve hours of daylight? Those who walk during the day do not stumble, because they see the light of this world. But those who walk at night stumble, because the light is not in them."

READER 3   After saying this, he told them, "Our friend Lazarus has fallen asleep, but I am going there to awaken him." The disciples said to him, "Lord, if he has fallen asleep, he will be all right." Jesus, however, had been speaking about his death, but they thought that he was referring merely to sleep. Then Jesus told them plainly, "Lazarus is dead. For your sake I am glad I was not there, so that you may believe. But let us go to him." Thomas, who was called the Twin, said to his fellow disciples, "Let us also go, that we may die with him."

READER 4   When Jesus arrived, he found that Lazarus had already been in the tomb four days. Now Bethany was near Jerusalem, some two miles away, and many of the Jews had come to Martha and Mary to console them about their brother. When Martha heard that Jesus was coming, she went and met him, while Mary stayed at home.

READER 1   Martha said, to Jesus, "Lord, if you had been here, my brother would not have died. But even now I know that God will give you whatever you ask of him." Jesus said to her, "Your brother will rise again." Martha said to him, "I know that he will rise again in the resurrection on the last day." Jesus said to her, "I am the resurrection and the life. Those who believe in me, even though they die, will live, and everyone who lives and believes in me will never die. Do you believe this?" She said to him, "Yes, Lord, I believe that you are the Messiah, the Son of God, the one coming into the world."

READER 2   When she had said this, she went back and called her sister Mary, and told her privately, "The Teacher is here and is calling for you." And when she heard it, she got up quickly and went to him. Now Jesus had not yet come to the village, but was still at the place where Martha had met him. The Jews who were with her in the house, consoling her, saw Mary get up quickly and go out. They followed her because they thought that she was going to the tomb to weep there.

READER 3   When Mary came where Jesus was and saw him, she knelt at his feet and said to him, "Lord, if you had been here, my brother would not have died." When Jesus saw her weeping, and the Jews who came with her also weeping, he was greatly disturbed in spirit and deeply moved. He said, "Where have you laid him?" They said to him, "Lord, come and see." Jesus began to weep. So the Jews said, "See how he loved him!" But some of them said, "Could not he who opened the eyes of the blind man have kept this man from dying?"

READER 4   Then Jesus, again greatly disturbed, came to the tomb. It was a cave, and a stone was lying against it. Jesus said, "Take away the stone." Martha, the sister of the dead man, said to him, "Lord, already there is a stench because he has been dead four days." Jesus said to her, "Did I not tell you that if you believed, you would see the glory of God?" So they took away the stone.

READER 1   And Jesus looked upward and said, "Father, I thank you for having heard me. I know that you always hear me, but I have said this for the sake of the crowd standing here, so that they may believe that you sent me." When he had said this, he cried with a loud voice, "Lazarus, come out!" The dead man came out, his hands and feet bound with strips of cloth, and his face wrapped in a cloth. Jesus said to them, "Unbind him, and let him go."

READER 2   Many of the Jews therefore, who had come with Mary and had seen what Jesus did, believed in him.

Reflection

LEADER   "W.W.J.D." are letters on bracelets to remind the wearer to ask "What would Jesus do?" In this passage we see several facets of Jesus that give direction to our own lives. First, he stays two days longer. Jesus could have quickly gone to his friend Lazarus; he could have been the first to console Martha and Mary; yet he chose what seemed like an uncaring response for the greater good of showing God's glory. Are there times in our lives when we need to do something that may appear uncaring, even unchristian, because of a higher good? Next, Jesus faced almost certain death by going to Bethany. Yet even the prospect of death didn't stop him from giving supreme proof of life-giving power and a sign of the final resurrection, as well as of the rising from sin to grace that takes place in every believer. This was a convincing sign in a gospel full of signs that were far more than wonder-working; the signs showed that Jesus was an emissary of the Father (cf. John 5:19–24). When are we emissaries of the Father? What are we willing to risk to be an emissary of God?

Then Jesus was emotionally moved by the death of Lazarus and the mourning taking place. He was not ashamed to let his weeping be seen. Are we willing to put emotion into living the Christian life? Do we show real concern for the persons we serve, or are we just doing our job? Do we let joy mark our faces when we experience a good liturgy? When others suffer, are we willing to cry with them? Do we refrain from quick-fix responses like "Everything will be all right"? Do we take the time to reiterate the problem we just heard; for example, "Yes, that must be very hard, and I empathize with you"?

Finally Jesus prayed publicly for the sake of the crowd. He let his confidence in God his Father be known. Are we willing to pray publicly? Do we ever say "I'll pray for you" when we hear of some problem? Do we ask a friend, "Could we pray about that now?" Do we let others know of our confidence in God; for example, by saying, "I know God answers our prayer"?

Activities (choose one)

1. Invite a speaker to talk on consoling the bereaved.

2. Come early to class on specified days for the rest of the school year to pray together. Begin by letting everyone share a particular concern, then pray about those concerns.

3. Try to attend all the liturgical services of the Sacred Triduum. If you have a special role, practice well. Ask the liturgy committee whether your class is needed to help decorate for Easter, pass programs, etc.

Closing Prayer

LEADER   Lord Jesus Christ, you taught us how to live and how to die and rise.

ALL   Be our words when we speak. Be our hands when we serve.

Be our voice when we pray. Be our mind when we think.

Be our strength when we act. Be our heart when we love.

Help us always and everywhere to do what you would do. Amen.

To Drink of the Cup Is to Share in the Death of the Lord

Theme

Partaking of the Blood of Christ means a covenant commitment to be what Jesus was: food for the life of the world.

Materials Needed

Bibles

Call to Prayer

LEADER Listen to these words as if Jesus Christ were speaking them to you right now. My dearest friend, long ago I shed my blood—for you. I was scourged and crowned with thorns—for you. I sweat drops of blood in utter agony—for you. I even gave up my life so that I could take on a new life—one that could be shared with you. You see, I love you so very much that I would do anything for you. (pause) I was wondering: would you do anything for me? (pause)

Reading (Matthew 26:26–30; 27:45–51, 54)

READER 1 While they were eating, Jesus took a loaf of bread, and after blessing it he broke it, gave it to the disciples, and said, "Take, eat; this is my body." Then he took a cup, and after giving thanks he gave it to them, saying, "Drink from it, all of you; for this is my blood of the covenant, which is poured out for many for the forgiveness of sins. I tell you, I will never drink of this fruit of the vine until that day when I drink it new with you in my Father's kingdom." When they had sung the hymn, they went out to the Mount of Olives.

READER 2 From noon on, darkness came over the whole land until three in the afternoon. And after three o'clock Jesus cried with a loud voice, "Eli, Eli, lema sabachthani?" that is, "My God, my God, why have you forsaken me?" When some of the bystanders heard it, they said, "This man is calling for Elijah." At once one of them ran and got a sponge, filled it with sour wine, put it on a stick, and gave it to him to drink. But the others said, "Wait, let us see whether Elijah will come to save him." Then Jesus cried again with a loud voice and breathed his last.

READER 3 At that moment the curtain of the temple was torn in two, from top to bottom.

The earth shook, and the rocks were split. Now when the centurion and those with him, who were keeping watch over Jesus, saw the earthquake and what took place, they were terrified and said, "Truly this man was God's Son!"

Reflection

LEADER   Having drunk of the blood of the new covenant, the apostles must now be ready to face death along with Jesus. Every gospel account of the institution of the Eucharist connects the Blood of Christ (which in Aramaic meant the whole person when death is anticipated) with the covenant. To drink of the cup is to share in the covenant sealed by the death of Christ. To drink of the cup means to accept death as the way to life, crucifixion as the way to resurrection. The apostles put themselves on the road to Calvary at the Last Supper (although their betrayal and fear would postpone their martyrdom many years). Our own reception of Holy Communion puts us on the road to Calvary.

The terms of the new covenant include being what Jesus was and doing what Jesus did. Jesus was Sacrifice. Are we willing to be a sacrifice? Would our willingness to give up things include the willingness to give up ourselves? Jesus was food for the life of the world. Are we willing to become "food" for others? At every Eucharist Jesus is diner and dinner. Are we willing to become diner and dinner?

Activities (choose one)

1. Our eucharistic Lord is food for the life of the world. In imitation of Christ, list ways you can be food for the life of the world.

2. Divide the entire reading of the Passion Narrative from Matthew's gospel into several sections. Have groups dramatize the section as it may have happened historically, then dramatize how people today are undergoing the passion in a similar way. Example: Dramatize the agony in the garden, then a hospital waiting room where parents are agonizing over a child during surgery.

3. Meditate on Jesus' imprisonment. Talk with Jesus in the prison.

Closing Prayer

LEADER   Lord Jesus Christ, we reluctantly admit that our salvation comes not only from partaking of your body and blood in weekly Mass attendance. We are saved by entering into your covenant of self-giving to the point of death.

ALL   Help us be willing to give ourselves as you did: body broken and blood poured out. This is scary, but we trust you, Jesus, for you are our friend and guide.

LEADER   Make us one with you in your saving death by our daily sacrifices.

ALL   Help us pick up our cross when we'd rather say "I don't wanna."

LEADER   Lead us to Calvary when we'd rather take a smooth road. Lead us to commitment when breaking promises is more convenient.

ALL   Lead us to the "blood of the covenant" when we have no way of seeing beyond suffering and death, for we trust in your resurrection. All shall be well: that is your promise, too. Amen.

Easter Sunday
Acts 10:34, 37–43; 1 Corinthians 5:6–8; John 20:1–9

"It Is the Lord!"

Theme

The resurrection is the church's claim to be an instrument of God's salvation in the world.

Call to Prayer

LEADER God our Father, as you raised your son Jesus from the dead, raise up among us people who will be able to show your love to the world.

ALL Help us realize how much you love us so that we can really believe that we are lovable.

LEADER Then let us reach out to those who think they are unlovable and cannot accept themselves.

ALL May your love spread to others through us.

LEADER Let love be so abundant that Christ is visible again.

ALL When people experience love, let them say, "It is the Lord!"

Reading (John 20:1–9)

READER 1 Early on the first day of the week, while it was still dark, Mary Magdalene came to the tomb and saw that the stone had been removed from the tomb. So she ran and went to Simon Peter and the other disciple, the one whom Jesus loved, and said to them, "They have taken the Lord out of the tomb, and we do not know where they have laid him."

READER 2 Then Peter and the other disciple set out and went toward the tomb. The two were running together, but the other disciple outran Peter and reached the tomb first. He bent down to look in and saw the linen wrappings lying there, but he did not go in.

READER 3 Then Simon Peter came, following him, and went into the tomb. He saw the linen wrappings lying there, and the cloth that had been on Jesus' head, not lying with the linen wrappings but rolled up in a place by itself. Then the other disciple, who reached the tomb first, also went in, and he saw and believed; for as yet they did not understand the scripture, that he must rise from the dead.

Reflection

LEADER One great joy of Easter was the knowledge that Christ was visible again. Peter, John, and Mary Magdalene were among the privileged ones to see the Lord! Up close or from a distance, on Easter morning and for several days thereafter, they would shout, "It is the Lord!" This shout of happiness became the early Christians' creed: "Jesus is Lord!" The reality of Easter and the meaning of this three-word creed express a totality. Easter isn't just rising from the dead; it's the whole mystery of resurrection, ascension and establishment as Lord, sending the Spirit, and, to a certain extent, the Second Coming. Resurrected, Jesus is no longer just the carpenter of Nazareth and itinerant preacher; he is the Christ whose resurrection is our claim to be instruments of his saving mystery to the world. It is our privilege to live the life of Christ so completely that when others experience church (ourselves along with all God's people), they can exclaim, "It is the Lord!"

Are others happy to have us around? Is there some character trait that needs improvement so that others will like us more? Why are social skills important if we are to be instruments of God's salvation to the world?

Activities (choose one)

1. In other times, the egg, symbol of the tomb, could not be eaten during Lent. When you eat Easter eggs, think of the open tomb, and reflect on your own openness to new things.

2. Listen to "Song of the Empty Tomb" from *The Song of Mark*, Marty Haugen (GIA Publications, 1995).

3. In quiet repeat in your mind and heart, "It is the Lord!" many times like a mantra. Be open to the blessings of the presence of the resurrected Lord.

Closing Prayer

LEADER Resurrected Lord, you appeared to the women and sent them to tell the good news;

ALL Help us proclaim the good news of Easter with the conviction that comes from knowing you as friend.

LEADER Redeemer of all, you gave us the Easter gift of peace;

ALL Teach us nonviolence, and keep our hearts in peace.

LEADER Giver of life, bless the springtime with abundant life.

ALL Help us rejoice and be glad, for this is the day the Lord has made.

LEADER Victorious Lord, teach us the winning ways of prayer and faith.

ALL   Let us run the journey of Easter more eagerly, giving new hope to the world by making Christ visible. Amen.

God, Just Tell Me It's OK

Theme

Like Thomas, we can make stupid mistakes that make us feel unworthy to be called disciples of Jesus; however, God is always there to tell us it's OK.

Call to Prayer

LEADER   Sometimes we get down on ourselves, God, and we feel as if we mean nothing to anyone, even you. We know this isn't true; deep down we know you care more about us than we could ever imagine. But we still wonder, "How could God love me after what I did?"

ALL   God, we praise and thank you that you love us without limit. Your love is such a great gift to us.

LEADER   Just knowing you are there, that your love is supporting us, keeps us going when everything else around us seems to go wrong.

ALL   When life is falling apart, help us feel your comfort, let us remember your concern, and give us the faith to love ourselves, for you have made us lovable. God, sometimes I just need to hear you say, "It's OK."

Reading (John 20:19–31)

READER 1   When it was evening on that day, the first day of the week, and the doors of the house where the disciples had met were locked for fear of the Jews, Jesus came and stood among them and said, "Peace be with you." After he said this, he showed them his hands and his side. Then the disciples rejoiced when they saw the Lord.

READER 2   Jesus said to them again, "Peace be with you. As the Father has sent me, so I send you." When he had said this, he breathed on them and said to them, "Receive the Holy Spirit. If you forgive the sins of any, they are forgiven them; if you retain the sins of any, they are retained."

READER 3   But Thomas (who was called the Twin), one of the twelve, was not with them when Jesus came. So the other disciples told him, "We have seen the Lord." But he said to them, "Unless I see the mark of the nails in his hands, and put my finger in the mark of the nails and my hands in his side, I will not believe."

READER 4   A week later his disciples were again in the house, and Thomas was with them. Although the doors were shut, Jesus came and stood among them and said, "Peace be with you." Then he said to Thomas, "Put your finger here and see my hands. Reach out your hand and put it in my side. Do not doubt but believe."

READER 5   Thomas answered, "My Lord and my God!" Jesus said to him, "Have you believed because you have seen me? Blessed are those who have not seen and yet have come to believe." Now Jesus did many other signs in the presence of his disciples, which are not written in this book. But these are written so that you may come to believe that Jesus is the Messiah, the Son of God, and that through believing you may have life in his name.

Reflection

LEADER   Thomas wanted Jesus to reveal himself. When he got what he wanted a week later, the reverse happened: Thomas wanted to reveal himself to Jesus. Although it's not stated in the gospel, one can imagine that Thomas knew it was the Lord before he ever put his hands in the nail marks. Nail marks were not necessary for Thomas' faith in Jesus, but they may have been necessary for his faith in himself. Thomas may have felt so bad about who he was that he wanted to be more known by the Lord. The opportunity to touch may have been a way of saying, "Put your arms around me, Jesus. Yes, call me to your side, but I don't need proof that you rose, just proof that you understand how afraid I was and how stupid and foolish and guilty I feel now. I don't really need to discover what a glorified body means; it's more important that I reveal myself to you. Just be with me, pray with me, free me from my fears, put your arm around me. Just tell me it's OK."

Are there times when you want to be really close to the Lord? How can you achieve this? Are there times when you feel too unworthy to be called a disciple of Jesus? What can you do at these times?

Activities (choose one)

1. Sit very close to a tabernacle. Pretend you are Thomas being embraced by Jesus. Don't say much mentally; just let Jesus in the Eucharist love you.

2. Discuss how teens (and adults) may sometimes do very foolish things. What foolish things should be avoided in the activities of spring, such as prom, school picnics, class trips? How can the immature and foolish be avoided?

Closing Prayer

LEADER   Please respond, "God, be with us."
When failure outweighs success... (Response.)

When troubles seem more numerous than good times... (Response.)

When we doubt ourselves and wonder about our worth... (Response.)

When temptations become too hard to resist... (Response.)

When parents and those in authority hold things against us... (Response.)

When prayer is the last thing we want to do... (Response.)

When cheating, stealing, and lying are the easy way out... (Response.)

When it seems, God, as if you don't care... (Response.)

When religious obligations are burdensome... (Response.)

When good deeds seem silly and goody-goody... (Response.)

When the school year seems long and summer vacation far away... (Response.)

When we need to hear "It's OK"... (Response.)

ALL   Amen.

God Waits to Be Asked

Theme

God waits to be asked for help. Don't miss an opportunity to ask and receive.

Materials Needed

Items to write invitations, Bibles, discussion questions for Emmaus walk

Call to Prayer

LEADER God, do you wait to be asked? Do you want to hear our trust and faith in you? Are you so polite that you wait for an invitation before you come into our lives? We come before you now with things that we need. Let us voice our needs. After each spontaneous petition, please add, "We invite you into this situation, Lord."
(Spontaneous petitions)

Reading (Luke 24:13–35)

READER 1 Now on that same day two of them were going to a village called Emmaus, about seven miles from Jerusalem, and talking with each other about all these things that had happened. While they were talking and discussing, Jesus himself came near and went with them, but their eyes were kept from recognizing him. And he said to them, "What are you discussing with each other while you walk along?" They stood still, looking sad. Then one of them, whose name was Cleopas, answered him, "Are you the only stranger in Jerusalem who does not know the things that have taken place there in these days?" He asked them, "What things?"

READER 2 They replied, "The things about Jesus of Nazareth, who was a prophet mighty in deed and word before God and all the people, and how our chief priests and leaders handed him over to be condemned to death and crucified him. But we had hoped that he was the one to redeem Israel. Yes, and besides all this, it is now the third day since these things took place. Moreover, some women of our group astounded us. They were at the tomb early this morning, and when they did not find his body there, they came back and told us that they had indeed seen a vision of angels, who said that he was alive. Some of those who were with us went to the tomb and found it just as the women had said; but they did not see him."

READER 3 Then he said to them, "Oh, how foolish you are, and how slow of heart to believe all that the prophets had declared! Was it not necessary that the Messiah should suffer these things and then enter into his glory?" Then beginning with Moses and all the prophets, he interpreted to them the things about himself in all the scriptures.

READER 4 As they came near the village to which they were going, he walked ahead as if he were going on. But they urged him strongly, saying, "Stay with us, because it is almost evening and the day is now nearly over." So he went in to stay with them. When he was at the table with them, he took bread, blessed and broke it, and gave it to them. Then their eyes were opened, and they recognized him; and he vanished from their sight.

READER 5 They said to each other, "Were not our hearts burning within us while he was talking to us on the road, while he was opening the scriptures to us?" That same hour they got up and returned to Jerusalem; and they found the eleven and their companions gathered together. They were saying, "The Lord has risen indeed, and he has appeared to Simon!" Then they told what had happened on the road, and how he had been made known to them in the breaking of the bread.

Reflection

LEADER What if the two disciples walking to Emmaus had not invited the stranger to stay for the evening? We would never have had this beautiful account of recognizing Christ in the breaking of the bread. In a similar way, what if others had not invited Jesus or made requests of him? What if the seasick apostles had not called out to the "ghost" walking on the water or wakened Jesus from his sleep during the storm? What if the ten lepers had not called out for pity? What if the synagogue leader had not begged Jesus for the life of his daughter? What if the woman with the hemorrhages had not touched the hem of Jesus' garment? What if the Canaanite woman had not begged for her daughter afflicted with a demon?

Could it have been that many other people of Jesus' day did not invite Jesus to help or come to their homes? Although many times Jesus takes the initiative in helping others, there are times that Jesus wants to be asked. The Emmaus story is one such time that we are taught to invite Jesus into our lives. Do you ever specifically invite Jesus into your life? How can this be done?

Activities (choose one)

1. Write an invitation to Jesus to ask for something you specifically need. Pray about the invitation, and expect a reply.

2. With one other person take an "Emmaus Walk." Talk about Jesus together. Imagine that Jesus is walking along with you. You may wish to discuss a particular gospel passage and prepared discussion questions.

Closing Prayer

LEADER   Walk beside us, Lord Jesus.

ALL   Come into our hearts and our homes.

Come into our athletic activities and fun.

Come into our places of work.

Come into our plans and dreams.

Come into our present and our future.

Come into our good deeds and service.

We need you, Jesus. Be with us where we are.

Amen.

We Belong to Christ

Theme

As sheep of his flock, we belong to Christ, the Good Shepherd.

Call to Prayer

LEADER   Let us pray Psalm 100.

SIDE 1   Make a joyful noise to the Lord, all the earth.

SIDE 2   Worship the Lord with gladness; come into his presence with singing.

SIDE 1   Know that the Lord is God. It is he that made us, and we are his; we are his people, and the sheep of his pasture.

SIDE 2   Enter his gates with thanksgiving, and his courts with praise. Give thanks to him, bless his name.

SIDE 1   For the Lord is good; his steadfast love endures forever, and his faithfulness to all generations.

Reading (John 10:1–10)

READER 1   "Very truly, I tell you, anyone who does not enter the sheepfold by the gate but climbs in by another way is a thief and a bandit. The one who enters by the gate is the shepherd of the sheep.

READER 2   "The gatekeeper opens the gate for him, and the sheep hear his voice. He calls his own sheep by name and leads them out. When he has brought out all his own, he goes ahead of them, and the sheep follow him because they know his voice. They will not follow a stranger, but they will run from him, because they do not know the voice of strangers."

READER 3   Jesus used this figure of speech with them, but they did not understand what he was saying to them. So again Jesus said to them, "Very truly, I tell you, I am the gate for the sheep. All who came before me are thieves and bandits; but the sheep did not listen to them. I am the gate. Whoever enters by me will be saved, and will come in and go out and find pasture. The thief comes only to steal and kill and destroy. I came that they may have life, and have it abundantly."

Reflection

LEADER   The image of the Good Shepherd may be so popular because it suggests a sense of belonging. We are the sheep, and the shepherd will take care of us, guide us, lead us to good pasture, and lead us home again. We need only to listen to his voice.

It is a sad fact that thousands of people across the globe feel that they don't belong. In the United States, for example, at least three children die every day from abuse or neglect, over three thousand drop out of high school on every school day, over eight thousand children are reported abused or neglected in a twenty-four-hour period, and there are 1.6 million abortions every year. We ourselves may know or be persons who are part of these statistics. The feeling of not belonging takes away one's identity and security, even when the feeling comes from less serious actions, such as not being asked to a dance or not getting elected as a class officer or not being chosen cheerleader. When we feel that we do not belong, we can remember that we are definitely part of Christ's flock; we belong to him.

How can we help persons who feel they do not belong? When we feel left out, what can we do to help ourselves? What should be done when you discover someone is abused or neglected, considers dropping out of school, or wants to run away from home?

Activities (choose one)

1. Plan a fund-raiser to help those who are abused or neglected.

2. Make efforts to have all students involved in end-of-the-year school activities.

3. Rewrite Psalm 23, starting with "The Lord is my shepherd," and make it pertain to your life.

Closing Prayer

LEADER   Help us hear your voice, Lord, that we may willingly respond.

SIDE 1   When you give us the grace to give up our selfishness and reach out to others with our time, talent, and resources, help us respond.

SIDE 2   When you make known to us the needs of others, give us the courage to meet those needs in the best way we can.

SIDE 1   When you put in our path opportunities to console, cheer, and comfort, help us make the effort in a way sensitive to the other person's feelings.

SIDE 2   When you see we are part of a group, team, or class, give us the strength to include everyone and to do our part without showing off or slacking off.

ALL   Good Shepherd, lead us along right paths. Amen.

Jesus, Our Way

Theme

The unity between God the Father and God the Son can be the unity between Jesus and ourselves if we have belief in Jesus as the way to the Father.

Materials Needed

Glass bowl, pieces of sponge, pitcher of water

Call to Prayer

LEADER   Lord Jesus Christ, you have promised us a dwelling place with you forever.

ALL   We thank you for this place and your loving preparation.

We thank you that you show us the way.

We thank you that you are the truth we seek.

We thank you that you are the life we live.

We thank you for empowering us when you went to the Father.

We thank you that you have promised us even greater works.

With these assurances our hearts will not be troubled; with you all is peace.

Reading (John 14:1–12)

READER 1   Jesus said to his disciples: "Do not let your your hearts be troubled. Believe in God, believe also in me. In my Father's house there are many dwelling places. If it were not so, would I have told you that I go to prepare a place for you? And if I go and prepare a place for you, I will come again and will take you to myself, so that where I am, there you may be also. And you know the way to the place where I am going."

READER 2   Thomas said to him, "Lord, we do not know where you are going. How can we know the way?" Jesus said to him, "I am the way, and the truth, and the life. No one comes to the Father except through me. If you know me, you will know my Father also. From now on you do know him and have seen him."

READER 3   Philip said to him, "Lord, show us the Father, and we will be satisfied." Jesus said to him, "Have I been with you all this time, Philip, and you still do not know me? Whoever has seen me has seen the Father. How can you say, 'Show us the Father'? Do you not believe that I am in the Father and the Father is in me?

READER 4 "The words that I say to you I do not speak on my own; but the Father who dwells in me does his works. Believe me that I am in the Father and the Father is in me; but if you do not, then believe me because of the works themselves. Very truly, I tell you, the one who believes in me will also do the works that I do and, in fact, will do greater works than these, because I am going to the Father."

Reflection

LEADER This passage is part of the Last Discourse given at mealtime in the final week of Jesus' life. In his farewell speech Jesus shows his disciples that the unity between Father and Son can be the unity between disciple and himself when he goes to the Father. The source of the unity is belief that Jesus is the way, the truth, and the life. The apostles come to the Father through Jesus whose words and works are those of the Father.

As summer vacation approaches we need to look at ways to keep in touch with Jesus when we no longer have these times of formal prayer. How can you fit more prayer into your day? What types of prayer would be most beneficial?

Activities (choose one)

1. In a clear bowl drop many pieces of sponge, each piece representing things that fill your day: study, work, recreation, sleep, meals, TV, music, phone calls, chores, and so on. When the bowl seems full, pour water into the bowl. What happens to the pieces of sponge? If the water is prayer and the sponge is the pieces of our lives, what is the connection between prayer and these activities?

2. Because there are few remaining classes, spend some time considering what topics or activities you still might want to do.

Closing Prayer

LEADER Jesus, we stand at a new millennium measuring time since you took on our human nature. From the time of your incarnation onward it has been our privilege to make you our home, even as you made our earth and our humanity your home.

ALL May the blessing of your love for us be with us today and with those we love. May the knowledge that we can always come home to you give us comfort. May your life be our way, your words our truth, and your love our way of living. Amen.

The Holy Spirit Is Energy

Theme

When the Holy Spirit gives guidance, the energy to follow that direction accompanies the gift. While we often refer to the Holy Spirit as Comforter or Guide or Consoler, we could also say the Holy Spirit is Energy.

Materials Needed

Nine paper flames

Call to Prayer

LEADER   Holy Spirit, creative love of Father and Son, renew us in love.

ALL   Holy Spirit, energy of Christ building up the kingdom, renew in us our spiritual energy. Holy Spirit, energizer of our souls, keep us spiritually alive and vibrant.

LEADER   Come, Holy Spirit, fill the hearts of your faithful,

ALL   and kindle in them the fire of your love.

LEADER   Send forth your Holy Spirit, and they shall be created,

ALL   and you shall renew the face of the earth.

Reading (John 14:15–21)

READER 1   Jesus said to his disciples: "If you love me, you will keep my commandments. And I will ask the Father, and he will you give you another Advocate, to be with you forever. This is the Spirit of truth, whom the world cannot receive, because it neither sees him nor knows him. You know him, because he abides with you, and he will be in you.

READER 2   "I will not leave you orphaned; I am coming to you. In a little while the world will no longer see me, but you will see me; because I live, you also will live. On that day you will know that I am in my Father, and you in me, and I in you. They who have my commandments and keep them are those who love me; and those who love me will be loved by my Father, and I will love them and reveal myself to them."

Reflection

LEADER Jesus Christ did not leave the apostles or us orphaned. He left us his spirit, which is the Holy Spirit. Prayer to the Holy Spirit is extremely powerful. We need to pray often to the Holy Spirit so that we can let the Spirit's gifts we received in baptism reach their full maturity. We may never stop growing in prayer, wisdom, kindness, understanding, courage, healing, tongues, joy, peace, patience, long-suffering, faith, hope, love, and many other charisms, or gifts. Using these gifts is the way we continue the life of Christ in the world. As we let the Spirit rain down upon our world, we will hasten the Second Coming, whose coming was implied already on Pentecost, for the coming of the Spirit implies the coming back of Jesus because of their Trinitarian life.

Does prayer to the Holy Spirit get you "fired up"? What miracles have you experienced through the power of the Holy Spirit? If the Spirit gives guidance, the Spirit will also give energy. If you feel in your heart that you should do a certain thing, the Spirit is there to help you accomplish it. God gives not only ideas but power. When have you ever experienced this?

Activities (choose one)

1. Ask someone gifted in charismatic prayer to lead your group in prayer to the Holy Spirit.

2. Finish this sentence: "The Holy Spirit is like . . ."

3. Write one gift of the Holy Spirit on each of the nine flames. On the nine days between Ascension and Pentecost, pray prayers to the Holy Spirit that ask for the particular gift.

Closing Prayer

LEADER Please respond, "We praise you, Jesus."
For the gift of your Holy Spirit… (Response.)

For your Spirit of understanding and courage… (Response.)

For your Spirit of wonder and awe… (Response.)

For your Spirit that energizes us… (Response.)

For your Spirit that gives healing to those who ask… (Response.)

For your Spirit who is a Giver of Peace… (Response.)

For your Spirit that fires us up… (Response.)

ALL Amen.

Mission Accomplished

Theme

Jesus finished the work his Father gave him to do during his life on earth. Are we accomplishing what God wants us to achieve during our lifetime?

Call to Prayer

LEADER   Heavenly Father, are you proud of us, your children?

ALL   God, it would be nice to know if we measure up in your mind. Are you pleased, or do you hold it against us when we mess up? Are we fulfilling your plan? Are we doing the work you want us to do? Are you glad you created us?

LEADER   (Close your eyes and imagine God speaking to you.) "I gave you my very own Son, because you were worth my very own Son. I gave you eternal life through Jesus, because it was my best gift, and you deserved the very best. I gave you my name, because I wanted you to be mine. Keep on doing my work, because I need you. I am very proud of you."

Reading (John 17:1–11)

READER 1   After Jesus had spoken these words, he looked up to heaven and said, "Father, the hour has come; glorify your Son so that the Son may glorify you, since you have given him authority over all people, to give eternal life to all whom you have given him. And this is eternal life, that they may know you, the only true God, and Jesus Christ whom you have sent. I glorified you on earth by finishing the work that you gave me to do. So now, Father, glorify me in your own presence with the glory that I had in your presence before the world existed.

READER 2   "I have made your name known to those whom you gave me from the world. They were yours, and you gave them to me, and they have kept your word. Now they know that everything you have given me is from you; for the words that you gave to me I have given to them, and they have received them and know in truth that I came from you; and they have believed that you sent me.

READER 3   "I am asking on their behalf; I am not asking on behalf of the world, but on behalf of those whom you gave me, because they are yours. All mine are yours, and yours are mine; and I have been glorified in them. And now I am no longer in the world, but they are in the world, and I am coming to you. Holy Father, protect them in your name that you have given me, so that they may be one, as we are one."

Reflection

LEADER   This passage, part of the High Priestly Prayer of Christ, seems to sum up the importance of Christ's life on earth. Jesus has fulfilled his mission to make God's name known, finished the Father's work, and given eternal life to his followers. Mission accomplished. Though spoken on a night of fear and farewell, this passage suggests that Jesus may have felt satisfaction in accomplishing his Father's will.

Do you ever wonder whether you are doing what you are meant to do? Do you ever ask yourself, "Does my life make any difference?" or "Why was I born?" These are healthy questions—when not asked in depression. Reflecting upon whether you are doing God's work and making his name known is important as a follower of Christ. Knowing you are doing the work of God should give much satisfaction. When have you done the work of God this past week?

Activities (choose one)

1. As summer vacation approaches, make a plan to do God's work throughout the summer months.

2. In groups discuss the following statements to see where you would put them on a continuum ranging from "Strongly disagree" to "Strongly agree," and how they fit into doing the work of God.

(a) I don't hide many things from my parents. I tell them the things they need to know.

(b) Mom says my activities are "rebellion," but I call them "exploration."

(c) Risky experimentation is part of being a teen and becoming one's own person.

(d) Teens are very different from their parents' image of them.

(e) Religion has little impact on the lives of teens compared to television and other media.

(f) Teens appreciate being left alone by their parents.

(g) Songs that glamorize drugs, alcohol, and violence are just music; there's nothing wrong in listening to them.

Closing Prayer

LEADER   Thank you, Heavenly Father, for the opportunity of knowing your Son Jesus.

ALL   Help us enter into Christ's work of glorifying you. Help us accomplish your work in everything we say and do. In this way our lives will take on more significance—as persons destined to show you, O God, to the world. Amen.

Peace Is Seeing the Whole Picture

Theme

Christ's gift to his apostles was peace. This peace is more than the absence of fighting; it is the ability to see ourselves and the world as whole.

Materials Needed

Globe or world map, modeling clay or finger paint

Call to Prayer

LEADER Wonderful God, we come before you to celebrate Pentecost. We praise and thank you for this feast celebrating the mystery of the continued presence of the Lord with us through the gift of the Spirit.

ALL Give us joy in the knowledge that final victory is within us. Help us to spread the Spirit's gift of peace to the whole world that everyone may experience the reign of God.

Reading (John 20:19–23)

READER 1 When it was evening on that day, the first day of the week, and the doors of the house where the disciples had met were locked for fear of the Jews, Jesus came and stood among them and said, "Peace be with you." After he said this, he showed them his hands and his side. Then the disciples rejoiced when they saw the Lord.

READER 2 Jesus said to them again, "Peace be with you. As the Father has sent me, so I send you." When he had said this, he breathed on them and said to them, "Receive the Holy Spirit. If you forgive the sins of any, they are forgiven them; if you retain the sins of any, they are retained."

Reflection

LEADER Pentecost made the apostles the "God Squad." The apostles, early Christians, and we ourselves complete many sendings as set forth in the Gospel of John: John the Baptist sent to herald the coming of Christ, Christ sent by the Father, the Spirit sent by Jesus, and Christ's followers sent into the world. The members of God's Squad give a message of peace that is more than the absence of fighting and tension; this peace is union with God. Such peace lets us begin to see the whole picture—the whole picture of bringing about God's reign through centuries of prophecy, the life of Jesus of Nazareth, and the Spirit's continuation that takes us into a new millennium.

The job of Pentecost is to try to see as God sees. And what does God see? God gazes into us and sees the whole person—a never-to-be-repeated image of God. God looks at our world of poverty and discrimination and sees the whole picture—a growing kingdom that is heading toward the fullness of God's reign. If we see with God's eyes, we will see ourselves and the world as beautiful, for the whole picture is beautiful. It is knowing ourselves and the world partially that clouds our vision to the goodness.

Instead of addressing each ethnic group, the apostles spoke to the "whole world" on Pentecost, and all understood. Unity and peace reigned when the apostles spoke to the people as one. How would relationships change in your families, school, places of work, and town if you looked at the whole group rather than individuals or isolated groups?

If you looked at yourself as a whole person, would you like yourself more? Do you tend to fixate on one aspect of yourself that you dislike? How can you integrate this one aspect of your body or personality with your whole being?

The apostles did not have books titled "How to Preach to the Nations." They had only the memory of Christ and the power of the Spirit. As a baptized and confirmed Christian, would you trust yourself enough to preach and teach God's Word?

Activities (choose one)

1. Reach out in prayer to the whole world and beg God's blessing upon each country that its citizens may be open to the message of Christ. To do this, close your eyes and point to a spot on a world map or globe. Spend a moment praying for that country's openness to God. (If you land on an ocean, pray for God's peace in the world or health for our planet.)

2. Using modeling clay or finger paint, portray that part of yourself you dislike. Rework that part into yourself in a more integrated way. As you work, think loving thoughts about the part you dislike. See how you can make what seems to be a minus a plus.

Closing Prayer

LEADER   Holy Spirit, help us in our weakness.

ALL   Help us to pray as often and as well as we are meant to.

LEADER   Holy Spirit, intercede for us and for our world.

ALL   With your help we will have peaceful wholeness.

LEADER   Holy Spirit, search our hearts and find goodness there.

ALL   Help us become more aware of our own goodness and less overcome by our imperfections.

LEADER   Holy Spirit, help us change into the person we are meant to be, persons who use all your gifts of faith, hope, love, kindness, helpfulness on a daily basis—not just when we feel like it.

ALL   Give us the courage to use your power, O Holy Spirit, within us. Amen.

God Couldn't Sit Still. We Shouldn't Either.

Theme

God's love is ongoing. The love God shares with us must be shared with others.

Materials

Tagboard, markers, candles, supplies to decorate candles

Call to Prayer

LEADER Holy, holy, holy is the Lord!

ALL God our Father, we praise you for the love that created our world and sent your Son.

God the Son, we praise you for showing such abundant love that you willingly died for us.

God the Holy Spirit, we praise you for your love in our hearts—a love so strong that we can't sit still, because we want to share it.

Reading (John 3:16–18)

READER 1 Jesus said to Nicodemus: "For God so loved the world that he gave his only Son, so that everyone who believes in him may not perish but may have eternal life.

READER 2 "Indeed, God did not send the Son into the world to condemn the world, but in order that the world might be saved through him. Those who believe in him are not condemned; but those who do not believe are condemned already, because they have not believed in the name of the only Son of God."

Reflection

LEADER God's love is so expansive that God had to do something with the love. God couldn't sit still! This love moved God to do something! God created a universe, populated a planet, set forth a plan in Adam and Eve, but still had to do more. So God sent the Son. And then the Son couldn't sit still. The Son cured and taught and established a kingdom, but still had more to do. So the Son sent the Spirit. And then the Spirit couldn't sit still. The Spirit shook the

Upper Room, gave the gift of tongues to the apostles, and came to every human being in baptism. And the love goes on. It's in us. Can we dare to sit still? Would we dare to stop the love? How can we keep the love of God moving?

Activities (choose one)

1. In the ancient church a piece of the consecrated bread from the Pope's Mass was used in subsequent liturgies. This piece of bread, called *sancta*, showed there is one Eucharist, and it keeps on going. Using this idea, write the word "LOVE" on tagboard. Cut the tagboard into enough pieces for everyone. Take these pieces home for the summer and use them as reminders to keep the love of God going. Challenge yourself to do one loving thing every day as part of the one great Love.

2. Decorate a candle with words and symbols that summarize the year's classes. (Candle stubs from the parish church may work.) Take the candle home and burn it when you seem far from the Lord. Remember how close God is to you.

Closing Prayer

LEADER   As the Father commissioned the Son, Jesus, and as Jesus commissioned the Holy Spirit, let us renew our baptismal commission to continue the loving work of God. Please respond "I will."

Since you have put on Christ in baptism, will you continue to show Christ to the world? (I will.)

Since you have often been fed with the Body and Blood of Christ, will you let your conduct be that of Christ? (I will.)

Since you have studied the life of Christ and know that discipleship costs, will you let yourself be sacrificed for the life of the world? (I will.)

Since God has loved you so much, will you try to love one another? (I will.)

Go in peace to love and serve the Lord in one another. (Thanks be to God.)

Of Related Interest...

Confirmed in the Spirit
Prayer Services for Confirmation
 Classes and Retreats
M. VALERIE SCHNEIDER, S.N.D.

The author believes that preparing high school students for confirmation should be a way of preparing them for life. Through ritual actions, Scripture readings, group prayers and reflections, these 20 prayer services help place the sacrament in a broader context and remind students that their commitment involves a lifelong responsibility. Includes 35 brief prayers for beginning or ending class and suggestions for additional activities. Perfect for teachers, catechists, pastors, DREs, youth ministers, sponsors, and parents too!

ISBN: 0-89622-655-7, 88 pp, $12.95

Teenagers Come and Pray!
Celebrating Milestones, Memorials,
 and Holy Days
MICHAEL D. AUSPERK

Here are 26 practical and pertinent prayer services for use throughout the school year which help modern teenagers find a sense of their own spirituality and responsibility as Christians amid the other demands in their lives. Topics covered include: beginning the school year, before a performance or competition, respect for life, on the death of a classmate or teacher, confirmation, and recovering from an addiction. This is the ideal book for catechists, youth ministers, religion teachers, and anyone struggling with the question of how to make religion more relevant to teenagers today.

ISBN: 0-89622-642-5, 112 pp, $12.95

Weekly Prayer Services for Teenagers
Lectionary-Based for the School Year
(Years A and B)
M. VALERIE SCHNEIDER, S.N.D.

These 37 prayer services are intended for junior and senior high school students, both in Catholic school and religious education settings. These services involve teenagers in a dramatic reading of Scripture, include questions for reflection and discussion, a time for communal prayer, and an activity. Themes cover generosity, forgiveness, sacrifice, discipleship, holiness, academics, baptismal commitment, liturgical seasons, and more.

ISBN: 0-89622-692-1, 104 pp, $12.95
Also available in Years B &C:
ISBN: 0-89622-732-4, 112 pp, $12.95

Prayer Services
for Young Adolescents
GWEN COSTELLO

Common concerns of 10-14 year-olds such as: peer pressure, clothes, smoking, drugs, faith, prayer, alcohol, profanity, sexuality, are addressed through group and private prayer and Scripture reflections. Particularly appealing is the guided meditation in each service.

ISBN: 0-89622-597-6, 80 pp, $9.95

Why Go To Mass
GREG DUES

This book helps answer the common teen question, "Why do I have to go to Mass?" The essays and values clarification activities give serious consideration to teenagers' feelings and outlook, rather than presenting an authoritarian stance. Each of eight chapters contains five to seven meaningfully illustrated worksheets for teenagers, as well as background and introductory materials for teachers and parents.

ISBN: 0-89622-604-2, 72 pp, $9.95

Available at religious bookstores or from:
⊠ TWENTY-THIRD PUBLICATIONS
P.O. BOX 180 • MYSTIC, CT 06355
1-800-321-0411 • E-Mail:ttpubs@aol.com